CAMBRIDGE ASSIGNMENTS IN MUSIC

General Musicianship

ROY BENNETT

CAMBRIDGE
UNIVERSITY PRESS

RANGES OF VOICES AND INSTRUMENTS

Voices

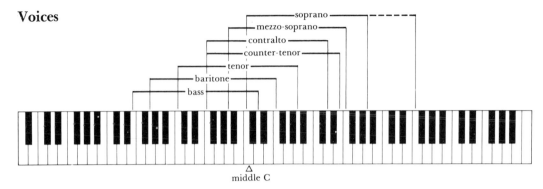

Strings

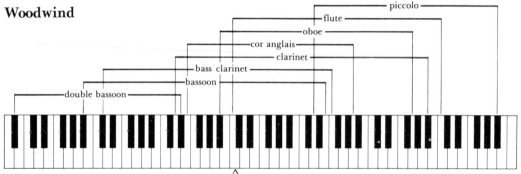

Woodwind

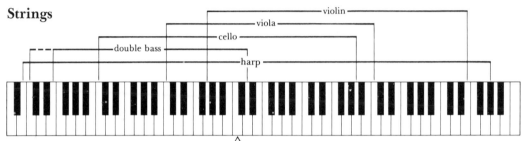

Brass

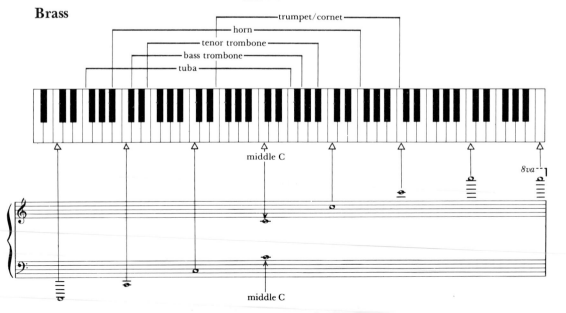

2

Contents

PART ONE: THE BASIC MATERIALS OF MUSIC

1
Some facts about sound

Every sound you hear is caused by something vibrating. The vibrations travel through the air as sound-waves which spread out in all directions at once. These eventually affect the sensitive membrane of the ear-drum, causing that to vibrate as well. The vibrations are then transformed into nervous impulses and transmitted to the brain, which identifies them as various types of sound.

Listen to the first two sounds recorded on the cassette.

In the first example, the vibrations set up a wave-form which has a constant, regular pattern (as represented in the first diagram on the left). We accept this as a 'musical' sound: a **note**, which has a distinct and definite pitch – in this case, a fairly high pitch.

In the second example, the vibrations of the crashing tray of wine-glasses produce a confused jumble of sound-waves of irregular pattern. We class these sounds, which lack definite pitch, as **noise**.

You may think noise has little to do with music – but in fact it can play a very important part. Many percussion instruments for instance (such as snare drum, cymbals, tambourine) make irregular vibrations, and so their sounds must be classed as 'noises' rather than 'notes'.

Listen to the next sequence on the cassette. As you hear each note, your brain is seeking out and identifying three main characteristics:

> 1 **Pitch** – how high, or how low, the note is
> 2 **Volume, or intensity** – how loud, or how soft, it sounds
> 3 **Timbre** – its special sound-quality, or tone-colour

We shall explore timbre in more detail later on; but for the moment let us investigate pitch and volume.

PITCH

The pitch of a note depends upon the *frequency*, or number, of vibrations per second. The higher the frequency, the higher the pitch of the note. If you pluck a string on a violin or a guitar you will be able to see, as well as hear, the vibrations – though they will be so fast that the movements of the string will appear as a blur. To sound the note we call 'middle C', the to-and-fro movements of the string must happen 261 times every second.

In any instrument where the sounds are made by causing strings to vibrate the frequency of the vibrations, and therefore the pitch of the note, depends upon the length, the thickness, and the tension (or tightness) of the string:

> the shorter the string
> the thinner the string } ⟶ the faster the vibrations,
> the tighter the string   and so the higher the pitch

violin

double bass

piccolo

bassoon

Length and size are also important to wind instruments, where the sounds are made by causing a 'column' of air to vibrate inside a hollow tube:

> the shorter the air column, the higher the note
> the longer the air column, the lower the note

The lowest-pitched sounds our ears can pick up have a frequency of 16 to 20 vibrations per second – for example, an extremely low organ note. The upper limit of human hearing is around 20,000 vibrations per second – a little higher than the squeak of a bat. Whales can pick up lower frequencies than humans; dogs can hear much higher ones. There is a whistle so high in pitch that no human can hear it. But dogs can hear it, and can be trained to obey its message.

VOLUME, OR LOUDNESS

Pluck a string on a violin or guitar: first gently, and then more firmly. The two notes you hear are of the same pitch, but the second is louder than the first. Pitch depends upon the frequency of the vibrations; but volume or loudness depends upon the strength of the vibrations – what we call the *amplitude*. The more force or energy applied in starting the vibrations, the greater the amplitude, and so the louder the sound.

soft ～～～～～～ *loud* ∿∿∿∿∿

You will sometimes hear the word 'decibels' mentioned in connection with the loudness of sounds in relation to each other. According to the scale of decibels, a sound measuring 1 dB (a single decibel) is extremely soft – just loud enough to cross our 'threshold of hearing'. A violin played quietly rates about 25 dB; a large orchestra playing at its loudest, around 100 dB. Sounds above 120 dB approach our 'threshold of pain' – for example, low-flying aircraft screaming overhead, or a motorbike with a faulty silencer roaring past.

Assignment 1

(a) What is the main difference between a *noise* and a musical *note*?
(b) Why does a piccolo sound higher than a bassoon?
(c) Give two reasons why a double bass string produces a lower note than a violin string.
(d) Why do the six strings of a guitar sound different pitches, even though they are all of the same length?
(e) What must a pianist do to vary the *volume* of his playing?

Assignment 2

Listen to the 'montage' of varied sounds recorded on the cassette. Identify as many as you can. Then make a chart to show the main characteristics of each sound. Your chart could begin like this:

Identification of sound	Noise, or notes	Pitch: high, middle, or low	Volume: soft, medium, or loud
trumpet	notes	high	loud
gust of wind	noise	middle/high	soft/medium

2
Musical notation: Pitch

'Notation' means the way in which sounds can be expressed on paper. The monks of medieval times were the first to write down sounds and indicate their pitch by using horizontal lines. At first, a single line was used. Later, more were added, making a stave of perhaps four, five, six, or even as many as eight lines.

The beginning of the medieval 'round' called 'Sumer is icumen in', written around the year 1250. The diamond-shaped notes are written on a six-line stave.

THE FIVE-LINE STAVE

Eventually, the five-line stave was agreed upon as being the most useful and also the easiest to read. The different notes are placed either on (*across*) the lines of the stave, or in the spaces between them. The higher a note's position on the stave, the higher its pitch:

Ex. 1

To name the pitch of notes, the first seven letters of the alphabet are used: A B C D E F G. After G, we begin again with A. Looking at the notes written in example 1, it is clear that the sounds steadily rise in pitch. But no clue is given to the precise pitch of any of these notes. For this, a sign is needed at the beginning of the stave

CLEFS

called a **clef** (meaning 'key'). A clef fixes the pitch of one of the five lines of the stave - and so gives the 'key', or clue, to the other lines and spaces. The two most commonly used clefs are the **treble clef** and the **bass clef**:

TREBLE CLEF AND BASS CLEF

The **treble clef** is used to show the pitch of notes lying above middle C. It is sometimes called the 'G' clef and in fact, originally, it was a decorative letter G. The treble, or G, clef circles around the second line of the stave - fixing this line as the note G:

became

The violin, flute, trumpet, and all other instruments of high pitch use the treble stave.

The **bass clef** is used to show the pitch of notes lying below middle C. This is sometimes called the 'F' clef since it was originally a letter F. The two dots are placed one on each side of the fourth line of the stave - fixing this line as the note F:

became

The cello, double bass, bassoon, tuba, and other instruments of low pitch use the bass stave.

This is what happens to the notes in Example 1 when first a treble (or G) clef, then a bass (or F) clef, is placed in front of them:

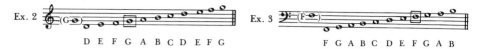

LEGER LINES

To write notes higher or lower in pitch than those shown above, extra short lines, called *leger lines*, are added above and below the stave. For example, middle C may be written on a leger line above the bass stave, or on a leger line below the treble stave. Here are bass and treble clefs brought together (as in music for piano) and linked by middle C written in both clefs (notice, though, that this is one and the same note on the piano keyboard - see diagram, bottom of page 2.)

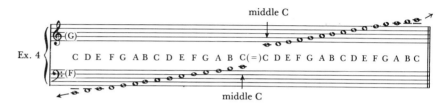

THE 'C' CLEF

There is a third kind of clef called the 'C' clef - originally a decorated letter C. Nowadays, this clef may be positioned on either the third or the fourth line of the stave. In either position, the line on which this clef is centred is fixed as middle C:

This C clef is often called the **alto** or **viola** clef. It is now used mainly in music written for viola.

This C clef is often called the **tenor** clef. It is used for upper notes of cellos, bassoons and tenor trombones.

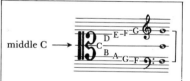

A stave with a C clef 'borrows' lines from the treble and bass clefs.

Assignment 3

Listen to the four instruments recorded on the cassette. Which *clef* would each one use for its music? (Name each instrument if you can.)

Assignment 4

Copy the following. Then write the letter-names beneath the notes.

Assignment 5

Write the letters which make up the words below as notes on
(a) the treble stave, (b) the bass stave, (c) the 'viola' C stave.
deaf, Ada, beg, café, feed, face, beef, cabbage, bad, fade, dead.

3
Musical notation: Rhythm

Music is divided, or 'measured', into *bars* by means of *bar-lines*. The end of a piece, or a section within a piece, is indicated by a *double bar* (really short for 'double bar-line').

By 'beating time' as we listen to music (perhaps by tapping a foot) we are marking the number of beats to a bar – the 'time' or 'metre' of the music. The first beat after a bar-line carries the strongest accent:

Duple time	(2 beats to a bar)	| ONE two | ONE two
Triple time	(3 beats to a bar)	| ONE two three | ONE two three
Quadruple time	(4 beats to a bar)	| ONE two Three four|ONE two Three four

Notice that in quadruple time, there are two accented beats – a strong accent on the first beat; a lesser accent on the third.

Music may be written in more than four beats to a bar – in which case each bar is really made up of some combination of two and three. For example, quintuple time (5 beats to a bar) may be counted as:
| ONE two Three four five | or as: | ONE two three Four five |

Assignment 6

Listen to the beginning of each of these pieces, and discover how many beats there are to each bar:
(a) Mozart: third movement from *Eine Kleine Nachtmusik*
(b) Bizet: Prelude to Act 2 of *Carmen* ('Les Dragons d'Alcala')
(c) Grieg: *Wedding Day at Troldhaugen*
(d) Holst: 'Mars, the Bringer of War', from *The Planets*

NOTE-VALUES

Notes written on a five-line stave are actually giving two kinds of information. The position of a note, according to the lines and spaces of the stave, indicates its **pitch**. The particular shape and design of a note indicates its **duration** – the length of time it lasts in relation to other notes.

For every kind of note there is a corresponding sign called a **rest** which indicates an equivalent length of silence. On the chart below, each note or rest lasts half as long as the one shown above it.

stem — hook
note-head

Name	Note	Rest	Value when each beat is a crotchet
semibreve	o	—	4 beats
minim	♩ or	—	2 beats
crotchet	♩ or	𝄽 or 𝄾	1 beat
quaver	♪ or	𝄾	$\frac{1}{2}$ (2 to a beat)
semiquaver	♪ or	𝄿	$\frac{1}{4}$ (4 to a beat)
demisemiquaver	♪ or	𝅀	$\frac{1}{8}$ (8 to a beat)

This is how the semibreve divides up into notes of shorter value:

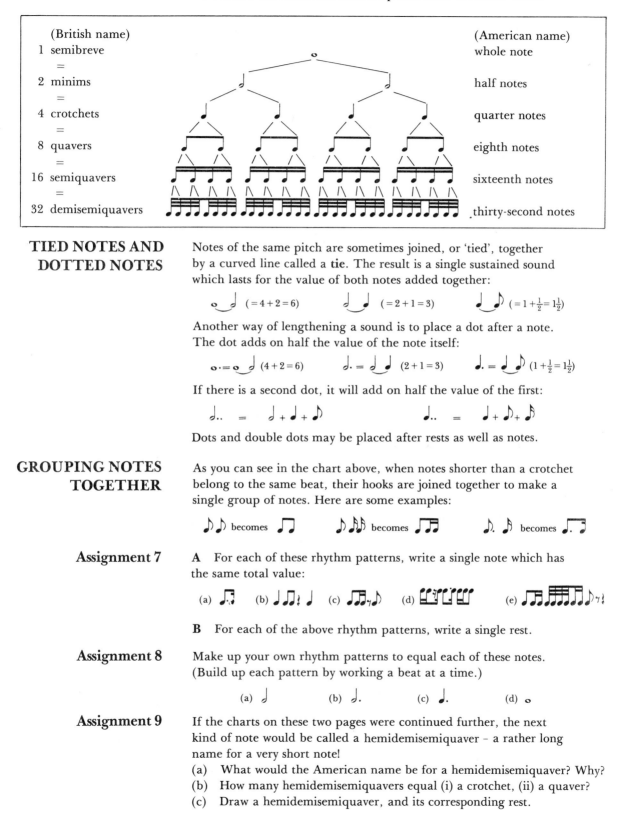

(British name)		(American name)
1 semibreve		whole note
=		
2 minims		half notes
=		
4 crotchets		quarter notes
=		
8 quavers		eighth notes
=		
16 semiquavers		sixteenth notes
=		
32 demisemiquavers		thirty-second notes

TIED NOTES AND DOTTED NOTES

Notes of the same pitch are sometimes joined, or 'tied', together by a curved line called a **tie**. The result is a single sustained sound which lasts for the value of both notes added together:

$(= 4 + 2 = 6)$ $(= 2 + 1 = 3)$ $(= 1 + \frac{1}{2} = 1\frac{1}{2})$

Another way of lengthening a sound is to place a dot after a note. The dot adds on half the value of the note itself:

$(4 + 2 = 6)$ $(2 + 1 = 3)$ $(1 + \frac{1}{2} = 1\frac{1}{2})$

If there is a second dot, it will add on half the value of the first:

Dots and double dots may be placed after rests as well as notes.

GROUPING NOTES TOGETHER

As you can see in the chart above, when notes shorter than a crotchet belong to the same beat, their hooks are joined together to make a single group of notes. Here are some examples:

becomes   becomes   becomes

Assignment 7

A   For each of these rhythm patterns, write a single note which has the same total value:

(a)   (b)   (c)   (d)   (e)

B   For each of the above rhythm patterns, write a single rest.

Assignment 8

Make up your own rhythm patterns to equal each of these notes. (Build up each pattern by working a beat at a time.)

(a)   (b)   (c)   (d)

Assignment 9

If the charts on these two pages were continued further, the next kind of note would be called a hemidemisemiquaver – a rather long name for a very short note!

(a)   What would the American name be for a hemidemisemiquaver? Why?

(b)   How many hemidemisemiquavers equal (i) a crotchet, (ii) a quaver?

(c)   Draw a hemidemisemiquaver, and its corresponding rest.

4
Time signatures

A **time signature** consists of two figures written one above the other at the beginning of a piece of music. This 'signifies' the *time* (the number of beats to each bar) which the composer is using. If each beat is a plain, simple note (that is, not a dotted note) the music is said to be in *simple time*. If, however, each beat is a dotted note, then the music is said to be in *compound time*.

In **simple time** each beat is divisible into halves. In **compound time** each beat (being a dotted note) divides into thirds. For example:

simple time: ♩ ♩ = ♫ ♫   compound time: ♩. ♩. = ♬ ♬

It is this dividing of the beat into three which often gives music written in compound time a dancing rhythm – lilting if the speed is moderate or slow, skipping if the music moves swiftly.

In a **simple time signature**, the top figure (as you can see from the chart below) always indicates the number of beats to each bar. The bottom figure represents a fraction of a semibreve, and indicates what *kind* of note is taken for the beat. Look at the chart on page 9 to see how, for instance, $\frac{3}{2}$ = three halves of a semibreve, and therefore three minims to each bar; or $\frac{4}{4}$ = four quarters of a semibreve, and therefore four crotchets to each bar; and so on.

Assignment 10

Write down a time signature to mean:
(a) simple duple time with a crotchet as the beat
(b) simple triple time with a minim as the beat
(c) simple quadruple time with a crotchet as the beat
(d) simple triple time with a quaver as the beat

A **compound time signature**, however, is rather different. In compound time, each beat is a *dotted* note, which divides into three – and here it is the number three which is important. While a compound time signature such as $\frac{6}{8}$ correctly tells us that there are six quavers to each bar, the *beat* is a dotted crotchet. A quaver is in fact worth only a third of this beat – so to find the number of beats to a bar we must divide the top figure of a compound time signature by three.

This chart includes the most commonly-used time signatures:

Composers sometimes write 𝐂 instead of $\frac{4}{4}$ (often called 'common time') and 𝄵 instead of $\frac{2}{2}$. 𝐂 is not in fact a capital standing for 'common'. In medieval times, triple time was shown by ○, a circle symbolising perfection; duple or quadruple by ⊂, a broken, or imperfect, circle.

Assignment 11   Write down a time signature to mean:
(a)   compound duple time with a dotted crotchet as the beat
(b)   compound triple time with a dotted crotchet as the beat

Assignment 12   How many beats to a bar does each of these time signatures indicate?
(a) $\frac{3}{2}$ (b) $\frac{2}{4}$ (c) $\frac{6}{8}$ (d) 𝐂   (e) $\frac{3}{8}$ (f) $\frac{5}{4}$ (g) 𝄵
For each signature: name, and draw, the note representing the beat.

Assignment 13   Supply a time signature for each of these scraps of tune. (Name each tune, too, if you recognise it.)

Assignment 14   Listen to the four extracts recorded on the cassette. For each one:
(a)   discover the number of beats in each bar;
(b)   decide whether the beats divide into twos (simple time) or threes (compound time);
(c)   write down a time signature to match.

5
Scales and keys

A **scale** (from a Latin word meaning 'ladder') is a series of notes moving upwards, or downwards, by step. Generally, the smallest step used in Western music is called a *semitone*. On the piano keyboard, the step from any note to its nearest neighbour is a semitone:

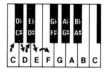

A step of two semitones (for example: C to D, or D to E) is a *tone*. (E to F, however, is a step of just one semitone.)

Notice that the black notes on the keyboard take their names from their neighbouring white notes, and that each has two names. If the black note between C and D is thought of as a semitone higher than C, it is called C sharp (C♯); but if it is thought of as a semitone lower than D, it is called D flat (D♭). These signs, called *accidentals*, are written in front of the notes which they alter:

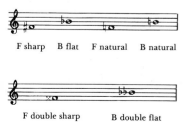

F sharp   B flat   F natural   B natural

F double sharp   B double flat

♯	sharp	raises the pitch of a note by one semitone
♭	flat	lowers the pitch of a note by one semitone
♮	natural	cancels a previous sharp or flat restoring a note to its original ('white-note') pitch
×	double sharp	raises a note by two semitones (= one tone)
♭♭	double flat	lowers a note by two semitones (= one tone)

Most music heard today is based upon two kinds of scale: the *major* scale, and the *minor* scale.

THE MAJOR SCALE

Play, or listen to, the white notes on the piano, climbing by step from middle C to the C an octave (eight notes) above. This is a **major scale** – in this case, since it begins and ends on C, called the scale of C major. Like all major scales, it is a mixture of tones and semitones (shown as T and S below) which are arranged according to a strict pattern:

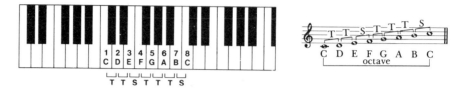

Notice that in a major scale, semitones must occur between the 3rd and 4th, and the 7th and 8th notes. A major scale can begin on *any* note, but this pattern of tones and semitones must be strictly kept.

C major, however, is the only major scale which can be played entirely on the white notes of the keyboard. To build other major scales we must make use of black notes, and name them accordingly.

For instance, in the scale of F major, to make the step of a semitone between the 3rd and 4th notes, we must use B *flat*. In the scale of G major, to make the step of a tone between the 6th and 7th notes, we must use F *sharp*.

F major scale   G major scale

NAMING THE NOTES OF A SCALE

We can refer to the degrees (the individual notes) of a scale by using numbers, by using their technical names, or their sol-fa names:

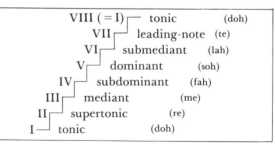

VIII (= I)	tonic	(doh)
VII	leading-note	(te)
VI	submediant	(lah)
V	dominant	(soh)
IV	subdominant	(fah)
III	mediant	(me)
II	supertonic	(re)
I	tonic	(doh)

THE MINOR SCALE

The most important difference between a major scale and a minor scale is that in a minor scale, the 3rd note is lowered by a semitone:

C major begins with a *major* ('larger') 3rd (= tone + tone):

major 3rd

C minor begins with a *minor* ('smaller') 3rd (= tone + semitone):

minor 3rd

There are two different patterns for the minor scale. One is called the *harmonic minor*; and the other, the *melodic minor*.

HARMONIC MINOR

The *harmonic minor scale* - so called because its notes are likely to be used in building chords and harmonies - lowers the 6th note as well as the 3rd. This makes a rather awkward step of a tone and a half (= three semitones) between the 6th and 7th notes:

C minor, harmonic:

MELODIC MINOR

The **melodic minor scale** - so called because its notes are likely to be used in building melodies - smooths away this awkward step by changing the 6th note when moving upwards, but lowering both the 6th and 7th notes when moving downwards:

C minor, melodic:

KEYS AND KEY SIGNATURES

If a piece of music is described as being 'in the key' of, say, G major, or C minor, then it will be built mainly from the notes of that particular scale. However, instead of writing the necessary sharps or flats as **accidentals** each time they occur, a composer lists them after the clef at the beginning of each line of music. This is the **key signature**, signifying which key he has chosen.

There is a key signature for each major key (though the one for C major, which needs neither sharps nor flats, is a 'blank'). Each major key, however, shares its signature with the minor key whose scale begins three semitones lower - in other words, on the 6th note (the submediant, or *lah*) of the major scale.

This chart shows the key signatures most often used. In each case, the white note is the tonic (the keynote, or *doh*) of the major key. The black note is the tonic of its *relative minor* - the minor key sharing the same signature. The leading-note (7th note, *te*) of each minor key is shown in brackets. This is 'extra' to the key signature and, where necessary, must be written in the music as an accidental.

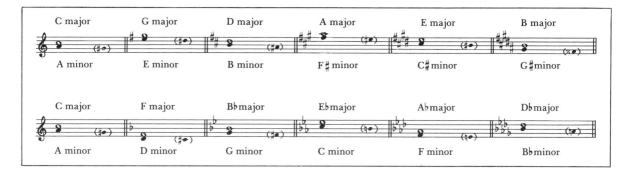

IDENTIFYING A KEY SIGNATURE

Notice that in a major key signature with sharps, the tonic (or *doh*) is a semitone above the last sharp. In a major key signature with flats, the tonic (*doh*) will be the last flat but one. But remember that each signature also belongs to a *minor* key. If your ear tells you that the music is in a minor key, check to see if the leading-note (*te*) is frequently written in the music with an accidental.

OTHER KINDS OF SCALE

There are many other kinds of scale on which music can be based. The most important are the *chromatic* scale, the *whole-tone* scale and the *pentatonic* scale.

The **chromatic** scale divides the octave into twelve equal steps of a semitone each:

The **whole-tone** scale contains no semitones but, as its name suggests, is built entirely from notes a whole tone apart.

for example: or:

A **pentatonic** scale uses five notes only from within the octave. Here are two examples (the second uses just the black keys on the piano):

(i)   (ii)

One famous tune built from a pentatonic scale is 'Auld Lang Syne'.

Assignment 15

Copy out, and name, the following notes. Then, according to each note's position on the piano keyboard, give an alternative name for the same sound. (For example: on the piano keyboard, F♯ = G♭)

Assignment 16

Listen to the eight extracts recorded on the cassette. Decide whether the music begins in a major key, or in a minor key; then write the correct key signature. (The tonic note, or *doh*, is given in brackets after each title.)

1. Tchaikovsky: *Barcarolle* (G)	5. Schumann: *Träumerei* ('Dreaming') (F)
2. Schubert: *Marche Militaire* (D)	6. Beethoven: *'Moonlight' Sonata* (C♯)
3. Grieg: *The Lonely Traveller* (B)	7. Macdowell: *To a Wild Rose* (A)
4. Mozart: *'Turkish' Rondo* (A)	8. Chopin: *'Revolutionary' Study* (C)

Assignment 17

A   Write the following as semibreves on the treble stave. Begin each example with the correct key signature.

1.   G major: tonic note, followed by subdominant
2.   D minor: dominant, supertonic
3.   B♭ major: leading-note, tonic

4.   A major: subdominant, tonic
5.   E minor: mediant, leading-note
6.   C minor: mediant, supertonic, dominant, leading-note, tonic

B   Rewrite the above examples, but using the bass stave.

6
Intervals

An **interval** is the distance in pitch between two notes. They may be sounded together; or one after another, as in a melody. An interval is identified by the number of *letter-names* it covers. Both top and bottom notes are included in the count. For instance, C-E is a 3rd since it covers 3 letter-names (CDE); C-F is a 4th (CDEF); C-G a 5th.

Ex. 1

unison 2nd 3rd 4th 5th 6th 7th octave

QUALITY

Besides number, intervals are also identified by *quality*. Five descriptions are used: perfect, major, minor, augmented, diminished. *Perfect* intervals are: unison, 4th, 5th, and octave.
2nds, 3rds, 6ths and 7ths may be *major* or *minor*. In Example 1, they are *major*. They are shown as steps of the *major scale*, which is used as a standard for measuring. (Any major scale might have been used.) If these major intervals are reduced by a semitone, they become minor:

Ex. 2

major 2nd minor 2nd major 3rd minor 3rd major 6th minor 6th major 7th minor 7th

If perfect or major intervals are increased by a semitone, they become *augmented* ('made larger'). (See Example 3.)
If perfect or minor intervals are reduced by a semitone, they become *diminished*. (See Example 4.)

How intervals become altered when raised or lowered by semitone:

augmented   augmented
↑   ↑
perfect   **major**
↓   ↓
diminished   minor
↓
diminished

Ex. 3

perfect augmented major augmented
4th   4th;   2nd   2nd

Ex. 4

perfect diminished minor diminished
5th   5th;   3rd   3rd

INVERSION OF INTERVALS

If the notes of an interval change position, the interval is said to be *inverted* ('turned upside down'). To find the new *number* of the interval, subtract the original number from 9. (So a 2nd becomes a 7th; a 3rd becomes a 6th; a 4th becomes a 5th.)

This is what happens to an interval's *quality* when it is inverted:

perfect remains perfect	augmented becomes diminished
major becomes minor	diminished becomes augmented
minor becomes major	

Ex. 5

perfect perfect major minor minor major augmented diminished diminished augmented
5th   4th   3rd   6th   3rd   6th   4th   5th   5th   4th

Assignment 18

A Name each of these intervals. First give the *number* (when counting, remember to include the lower note); then the *quality*. Take the lower note to be the tonic (*doh*) of a major scale. Then decide whether the upper note occurs in that scale (in which case the interval will be either perfect or major) or whether it has been raised or lowered.

(a) (b) (c) (d) (e) (f) (g) (h) (i) (j) (k)

B Invert, and then re-name, each of the intervals given above.

7
Italian terms

Italian composers were the first to write 'instruction' words at certain points in their music. Composers of other countries soon copied this idea – mostly choosing to use Italian as well, so that this has become the world-wide 'musical language'.

Here are some of the more common Italian terms which composers use:

A   Terms connected with **tempo** (speed, or pace)

grave serious, grave – usually very slow *lento* slow *largo* broad, slow *larghetto* rather broadly *adagio* leisurely – usually quite slow *andante* ('easy-going') at a walking pace *andantino* not as slow as *andante* *moderato* moderately *allegretto* not as fast as *allegro* *allegro* ('cheerful') fast *vivace* full of life *presto* very fast *prestissimo* as fast as possible	Terms marking a **change** of tempo: *accelerando* (*accel.*) getting quicker *stringendo* hurrying *allargando* broadening *rallentando* (*rall.*) getting slower *ritardando* (*rit.*) holding back *ritenuto* (*riten.*) held back *meno mosso* less moved, slower *più mosso* more moved, quicker *a tempo* or *tempo primo* return to the original speed

Sometimes, as well as (or instead of) a tempo marking expressed in Italian words, composers give a metronome marking. A metronome (invented by a friend of Beethoven's called Maelzel) ticks away the number of beats to a minute at any given speed. For example:

M.M. (Maelzel's metronome)   ♩ = 120

means there will be 120 crotchet beats per minute (or 2 per second).

B   Dynamic markings, indicating **volume** or **intensity**

pianissimo (*pp* and *ppp*) very soft *piano* (*p*) soft *mezzo piano* (*mp*) moderately soft *mezzo forte* (*mf*) moderately loud *forte* (*f*) loud *fortissimo* (*ff* and *fff*) very loud	*fp* loud, suddenly followed by soft *crescendo* (*cresc.*) getting louder *decrescendo* (*decresc.*) getting softer *diminuendo* (*dim.* or *dimin.*) getting softer *sforzando* (*sf* or *sfz*) and *forzato* (*fz*) forcing the tone, accenting the note

To many of the above terms, other words may be added such as:

molto much, very (*molto vivace* very lively)

assai very (*allegro assai* very fast)

ma non troppo, but not too much (*allegro ma non troppo* fast
    but not too much)

più more (*più lento* more slowly)

meno less (*meno forte* less loud)

poco a poco little by little (*poco a poco crescendo* getting
    louder little by little)

subito suddenly (*subito piano* suddenly soft)

agitato agitated
animato animated
appassionato passionately
ben well (ben marcato well
    marked)
brillante brilliantly
cantabile in a singing style
con with (con brio with
    vigour; con fuoco with fire;
    con moto with movement;
    con spirito with spirit)
deciso with decision, firmly
divisi divided
dolce sweetly
doloroso sorrowful
energico with energy
espressivo with expression
giocoso playful, humorous
giusto just, exact (tempo
    giusto at the exact speed)
glissando sliding
grazioso graceful
legato smoothly
leggiero lightly
maestoso majestic
martellato hammered
marcato marked
mesto sad
misterioso mysterious
ped (pedale) use the sustain-
    ing pedal on the piano

pesante heavily
piacevole pleasingly
pizzicato plucked (cancelled
    by arco bowed)
risoluto resolutely
rubato ('robbed'), at a
    flexible speed
scherzando jokingly,
    playfully
semplice in a simple way
sempre always
senza without
simile the same, similarly
sordino mute (con sordini
    with mutes; senza sordini
    without mutes)
sostenuto sustained
sotto voce ('under the
    voice'), softly
staccato detached, short
tacet be silent
tenuto held
tranquillo tranquil, calm
tre corde ('three strings'),
    release the soft pedal on
    the piano
tutti everybody plays
una corda ('one string'),
    depress the soft pedal on
    the piano
vivo lively

Assignment 19   As you listen to the beginning of each of these pieces, note down:
    (i)   an Italian term to indicate the tempo of the music;
    (ii) a dynamic marking;
    (iii) an Italian term (or terms) to describe the style or mood.
If there is any significant *change* of tempo, dynamics, style or mood,
suggest which Italian words or letters might be written in the music
to indicate this change.
(a)   Bizet: Prelude to Act I of *Carmen*
(b)   Verdi: Prelude to Act I of *La Traviata*
(c)   Mendelssohn: *Scherzo* from the incidental music to Shakespeare's
        'A Midsummer Night's Dream'
(d)   Wagner: Overture to *The Mastersingers*
(e)   Mozart: second movement from Piano Concerto No. 21 in C (K467)
(f)   Prokofiev: 'Romeo at Juliet's Tomb' from *Romeo and Juliet*
(g)   Grieg: 'In the Hall of the Mountain King' from *Peer Gynt*

8
Signs, symbols and abbreviations

Besides using Italian words and phrases, composers also use certain signs and symbols as a kind of 'musical shorthand', giving performers information in the briefest possible way about how the music is to be played. Here are explanations of some of the musical signs and symbols which are most often used:

———————	sign for *crescendo*, meaning 'getting louder'
———————	sign for *diminuendo*, meaning 'getting softer'
‖: :‖	repeat marks; :‖ means repeat from the previous pair of dots (or, if there is none, from the beginning of the piece)
⌐1. ⌐2.	'1st time' and '2nd time' at the end of a repeated section. First time, play the bar(s) marked ⌐1. ; but in the repeat, go straight to ⌐2.
D.C.	short for *da capo*, meaning repeat 'from the beginning'
Dal segno 𝄋	repeat 'from the sign'
Fine	'end'; *da capo al fine* means 'repeat from the beginning, then end at the word *fine*'
⌢	a pause sign written above or below a note or rest indicates that it should be held for longer than its normal value
⁒	repeat previous bar of music
G.P.	general pause (to be observed by all performers taking part)
8va--- 8va---⌋	passage to be performed an octave higher, or an octave lower, than written (this avoids using many leger lines)
con 8	the note one octave below is to be played at the same time as the written note

	sign for *arpeggio* ('in harp fashion'): play the notes of the chord one after another, beginning with the lowest
	a curved line ('slur') above or below notes of different pitch means join these notes together smoothly (*legato*)
	dots above or below notes mean make these notes short and detached (*staccato*)
	'wedges' above or below notes mean make these notes *very* short and detached
	sign for *tenuto* ('held'): slightly stress the note, then hold it for its full value
	sign for 'triplet': three notes to be played or sung evenly in the time of two notes of the same kind
	arrowheads above or below notes to indicate attack, accent, or emphasis
Op.	short for *opus*, meaning 'work' (e.g. Op. 10 No. 2 means the piece is the second item of the tenth work which the composer wrote)
a 2	this has at least two meanings: (a) in orchestral string music, (*divisi*) *a 2* means instruments in that section divide into 2 groups, taking one note each; (b) for other orchestral instruments (such as trumpets, flutes) *a 2* means 2 instruments play the same note(s) in unison

9
Ornaments

Ornaments (or **grace notes** as they are sometimes called) are 'extra' notes used to decorate a melodic line. They may appear as very small notes printed among the main notes of a melody; or they may be indicated by special signs - again a kind of 'musical shorthand'.

The chart below includes the ornaments you are most likely to find, together with explanations of how they may be performed. However, at least two important factors are involved. Performances of an ornament may differ according to (a) the period in the history of music when the piece was written and (b) the speed of the music.

For example, a trill in a piece by Bach (18th century) will not be exactly the same as a trill in a piece by Chopin (19th century) - though both will essentially consist of the alternation of the main written note with the note above it. As far as speed is concerned, a trill in slow music will take more notes than a trill in fast music.

tr or *tr*	*trill* (*occasionally called 'shake'*)	essentially, the alternation of the main written note with the note above it	
	upper mordent (*from Italian, meaning 'biting'*)	main note, note above, main note again	
	lower mordent	main note, note below, main note again	
	appoggiatura (*a 'leaning' note*)	usually steals half the value of the main note; often two-thirds of a dotted main note	
	acciaccatura (*a 'crushed' note*)	played quickly: usually on the beat, sometimes just before it	
	turn	essentially, 4 notes: note above, main note, note below, main note	
	inverted turn	note below, main note, note above, main note	

Special Assignment A

This Special Assignment consists of seven varied extracts of music, each with an accompanying set of questions. Your assignment here is to listen to each extract three or four times, discovering answers to the questions as you go along.

Here are some hints to help you:

Before the first hearing of an extract, examine the melody-line score and carefully read through all the questions so that you will have some idea of what you are expected to discover from the music.

In some questions, you will need to *listen* for an answer. Decide which questions these are, then plan your listening so that before each hearing of the music, you know what to listen *for*. Try to save the final hearing of the music to check these answers.

In other questions you will be able to discover answers by investigating the melody-line score. Work on these questions *between* hearings of the music.

1 Symphony No. 9 in C major   Schubert (1797-1828)

1. Which of these dynamic markings should be written below bar 1 of this music?

    p   *mf*   *f*   *ff*

2. One of the figures is missing from the time signature. What should the complete time signature be?

3. Choose one of the following tempo markings to match this music, then give its English meaning:

    lento;   andante;   presto.

4. Draw each kind of note-value used in this tune.

5. Make a list, arranging your note-values in the order of shortest to longest. Then name each one, and give its value in relation to the beat.

6. Name another composer who lived at the same time as Schubert.

2 **Second Movement from the 'Pathétique' Sonata**

Beethoven (1770-1827)

1. Which of these Italian terms best matches this music?

   adagio cantabile; *allegro appassionato*; *presto con fuoco*.

2. How many beats to each bar are there in this piece?

3. What is each beat worth?

4. What does the letter *p* mean, below bar 1? For which Italian word is this an abbreviation?

5. Which of these Italian words describes the way this melody is played?

   staccato; *legato*.

6. Beethoven also asks the pianist to play *dolce*. What does this mean?

7. Give the name, and also the value, of each of these notes:
   - (a) 1st note of bar 2;
   - (b) 2nd note of bar 4;
   - (c) last note of bar 7;
   - (d) last note of bar 11.

8. In which bar does the pianist play triplets? What is a triplet?

3 **'The Death of Åse' from *Peer Gynt***

Grieg (1843-1907)

Andante doloroso (♩ = 50)

1. Explain Grieg's tempo marking: *andante doloroso*.

2. Which section of the orchestra plays this music?

3. Which of these words should be printed below bar 1?

   pizzicato; *con sordino*; *una corda*.

4. How many beats to each bar has this music? Which note-value is used for the beat?

5. Choose a dynamic marking for the beginning of bar 4:

   pp   *mf*   *ff*

6. Explain: ♩ = 50, given in brackets after the tempo marking.

7. Is this music in a major key, or a minor key? Name the key. (The accidental at the beginning of bar 8 is in fact the leading-note of this key.)

8. Name any other composition by Grieg which you have heard.

1. Which of the following Italian phrases matches this music?

   lento doloroso;   *allegro con fuoco;*   *allegretto grazioso.*

2. In which key is this music written?

3. Explain the time signature which Haydn gives this Minuet.

4. Give the letter-names for the first two notes of the melody.

5. Explain the curved line drawn below these two notes.

6. Is the interval formed by these first two notes:

   a perfect 4th;   a major 3rd;   or a minor 3rd?

7. Give the meaning of each of these signs and ornaments:

   :|| ⅄   ♪   *tr*   *3*

8. Name another composer who lived at the same time as Haydn.

5 *Nocturne,* **Opus 9 No. 2**   Chopin (1810-1849)

1. Explain the meaning of *espressivo dolce.*

2. Choose an Italian word to match this style of playing:

   legato;   *staccato.*

3. Suggest a dynamic marking for the beginning of the melody.

4. Explain: ⟶ ⟵. Give an Italian word to match each sign.

5. Give the letter-names for the second and fourth notes of bar 8.

6. Is this music in a major key, or a minor key? Name the key.

7. Name these ornaments which Chopin uses to decorate his melody:

   ∾   ⋙   *tr*   ♪

8. This *Nocturne* (meaning 'night-piece') is in compound time.
   (a) How many beats are there to each bar?
   (b) What note-value is used for the beat?

9. What does Opus 9 No. 2 mean?

10. Mention titles of other pieces by Chopin which you have heard.

6 Variation 9 ('Nimrod') from *Enigma Variations*   Elgar (1857-1934)

1. Explain the tempo marking which Elgar uses.
2. The time signature is missing from this music. What should it be?
3. What does *diminuendo* mean? Which Italian term would mean precisely the opposite?
4. This music is mainly played by one section of the orchestra. Which?
5. In which bar do instruments from another section join in?
6. What interval is made by the two notes bracketed in bar 3?
7. In which other bars does this same interval appear?
8. Name both the pitch and value of the 3rd and 4th notes in bar 7.
9. What nationality was Elgar?
10. Name any other compositions by him which you have heard.

7 Gavotte from Violin Sonata No. 10   Corelli (1653-1713)

1. Suggest an Italian term to describe the tempo of this music.
2. In which key is this Gavotte?
3. Name the key which is the relative minor – the minor key which shares the same key signature.
4. How many beats to each bar has this music? What note-value is used for the beat?
5. Write Corelli's time signature in another way.
6. Describe the interval formed by the first two notes of bar 3. In which other bars does this same interval appear?
7. Name the shortest note-value which Corelli uses in this music.
8. Name the longest note-value used. What is this note worth in relation to the beat?
9. Which of these technical names describes the last note of the tune?
     tonic;   subdominant;   dominant;   leading-note.
10. Give the technical name for the first note of the tune.
11. Explain the curved line joining the last note of bar 7 to the first note of bar 8.
12. Name two composers who lived at the same time as Corelli.

Special Assignment B

As you can see, a great deal of information is missing from these four melody-line scores. Your assignment here is first to make a copy of each score. Then, while listening to each extract four or five times, discover the missing pieces of information which are required, and add them to your own score.

Read through all questions very carefully before you begin to listen.

1 **Intermezzo from _L'Arlésienne_ Suite 2**   Bizet (1838-1875)

1. Complete the time signature for this music by adding the missing figure to your score.
2. After the Italian tempo marking, write the English meaning in brackets.
3. Above each note in bar 1 and bar 4, add a sign to mean 'attack with emphasis'.
4. Below bar 1, add a suitable dynamic marking chosen from this list:
    pp   mp   mf   ff
5. Write another dynamic marking below bar 5.
6. Add a rest at the end of bar 4 to make this a complete bar.
7. At the beginning of this tune, all the instruments play in unison. Write the word _harmony_, in brackets, below the first bar where chords are played.

2 **Trumpet Voluntary**   Jeremiah Clarke (c1674-1707)

1. Choose one of these time signatures, and add it to your score:
    $\frac{2}{4}$ $\frac{3}{4}$ **C** $\frac{4}{2}$ $\frac{6}{8}$
2. Below the first note, write a suitable dynamic marking.
3. An ornament is missing from bar 1. Add the sign to your score.
4. Add the same sign anywhere else where this ornament is played.
5. Write a suitable tempo marking on your score, chosen from this list:
    Adagio pesante   _Andante cantabile_   _Allegro maestoso_
6. At bars 2 and 3, write the rhythm of the tune, below the stave.
7. Add a rest to bar 8 to make this a complete bar.

3 Prelude in A major, Opus 28 No. 7 Chopin (1810-1849)

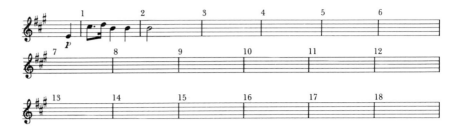

1. This piece is in fact shorter than the number of blank bars shown. Draw a double bar-line to show where the music actually ends.

2. The time signature is missing. Add this to your score.

3. Which of these tempo markings matches the speed of this music?
    Largo   *Andantino*   *Allegro molto*
    Add your choice above the beginning of your score.

4. How many times during this piece is this rhythm heard?

    Write your answer below bar 2.

5. In one bar, the pianist 'spreads out' the notes of a chord. Draw the sign which would instruct him to do this, at the beginning of the bar. And add a dynamic marking below.

6. Below the final bar of the piece, write the dynamic marking which means 'very soft'. And below the previous bar, give an indication that the music is 'getting softer'.

4 Theme from the Fourth Movement of the 'Trout' Quintet Schubert (1797-1828)

1. Add a suitable tempo marking to the beginning of your score.

2. Add a dynamic marking below the first note of the melody.

3. Which instrument plays this melody? Write its name below bar 1.

4. In which key is this music? Write your answer below the signature.

5. Fill in the missing time signature.

6. At bars 5 and 6, write the rhythm of the melody, below the stave.

7. At bar 16, add the ornament which is missing.

8. The melody ends on the tonic note, held for one-and-a-half beats. Add this note to your final bar.

10 Melodic and rhythmic devices

A composer may use various melodic and rhythmic devices – what we might describe as musical 'tricks of the trade' – to add interest and variety to a musical idea, or perhaps to extend or develop it in some way. The most important of these devices are illustrated below, based on this musical idea (taken from the opening of Beethoven's Third Piano Concerto):

DECORATION

Here, the melody is *decorated* or varied by the addition of ornaments and other extra notes:

SEQUENCE

A phrase of the melody may be immediately repeated at a slightly higher or lower pitch. This is called *sequence*:

IMITATION

One vocal or instrumental part sets off with a snatch of melody, then is immediately *imitated*, or copied, by another part bringing in the same tune:

If a complete melody is strictly imitated in this way, the result is a *canon* or *round* (as, for example, *Frère Jacques*).

INVERSION

The tune may be *inverted* – 'turned upside down' – so that intervals rising in pitch in the original version now fall, and vice versa:

AUGMENTATION

The melody may be drawn out by using notes of longer value. This is called *augmentation*:

DIMINUTION

Or the composer may use *diminution* – presenting the melody in notes of shorter value:

OSTINATO

A melodic, or rhythmic, fragment may be repeated over and over again as an *ostinato* (Italian: 'obstinate'):

SYNCOPATION

By using *syncopation*, the composer alters in some way the expected stress of the beats in a bar – perhaps by placing a rest on a strong beat, or placing an accent on a weak beat:

Assignment 20

Play or listen to this tune (borrowed from the Finale of Beethoven's Fifth Symphony):

In each of these examples, identify the melodic or rhythmic device which is used to treat the above tune:

Assignment 21

Try your own skill at using some of these musical devices. Take the tune below as your basic material and treat it, in turn, by:
(a) augmentation; (b) diminution; (c) inversion; (d) decoration.

Afterwards, play over your examples, making any adjustments which may seem necessary.

11
Chords and triads

Two or more notes sounding at the same time make a **chord**. A **triad** is a chord of three notes, built upon a main note, which is called the **root**, together with the notes which form a 3rd and a 5th above it:

Ex. 1

A triad can be built upon each note of any scale:

Ex. 2 In C major

I II III IV V VI VII VIII (= I)

Ex. 3 In A minor

I II III IV V VI VII VIII (= I)

MAJOR AND MINOR TRIADS

The two main kinds of triad are called *major* and *minor*. Each is named according to the kind of 3rd it contains. Both contain a perfect 5th.

Ex. 4

C major triad

major — perfect
3rd — 5th

A minor triad

minor — perfect
3rd — 5th

AUGMENTED AND DIMINISHED TRIADS

The two remaining kinds of triad are called *augmented* and *diminished*, and each of these is named according to the kind of 5th it contains. An augmented triad is a major triad whose 5th is raised a semitone. A diminished triad is a minor triad whose 5th is lowered a semitone.

Ex. 6

augmented triad on C

major — augmented 5th
3rd

Ex. 7

diminished triad on D

minor — diminished
3rd — 5th

ROOT POSITION AND INVERSION

All the examples above show triads in their **root position** – the note which is the root appears as the bass, the lowest-sounding note. Any triad or chord arranged so that a note other than the root is in the bass is said to be 'in inversion'. In **first inversion**, the 3rd will be the lowest note. In **second inversion**, the 5th will be lowest.

Ex. 8

root position 1st inversion 2nd inversion

root position: 5th / 3rd / root
1st inversion: root / 5th / 3rd
2nd inversion: 3rd / root / 5th

Assignment 22

Name each of these triads. Say which position each one is in – root position, first inversion, or second inversion.

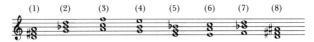

(1) (2) (3) (4) (5) (6) (7) (8)

Assignment 23

(a) Write these triads, in root position:

1. G major   4. A major   7. An augmented triad on F
2. B flat major   5. B minor   8. A diminished triad on C
3. D minor   6. C minor

(b) Now write the same triads (i) in first inversion, (ii) in second inversion. (Take as your guide the steps shown in Example 8, above.)

PRIMARY TRIADS

Of the seven triads built on the notes of any scale (see Examples 2 and 3, opposite) three are more important than the rest. In the same way as we speak of 'primary colours', we call these **primary triads**. They are the triads built on these three degrees of any scale:

tonic (I) • subdominant (IV) • dominant (V)

Here, for example, are the primary triads in C major and C minor. (Notice that in the minor key the leading-note is raised a semitone.)

Ex. 9

Assignment 24

Write out the primary triads in these keys:
(1) D major   (2) D minor   (3) B flat major   (4) G minor

CHORDS FROM TRIADS

The three notes of a triad may be used to build up a fuller-sounding chord by 'doubling' one or more of the notes at a higher or lower octave. These chords are built entirely from the C major triad:

Ex. 10

a) **Handel** (for voices)   b) **Mozart** (for piano)   c) **Beethoven** (for orchestra)

Extra notes may be added to a basic triad so that a more complicated chord may be built from it. For example, in C major, the notes of the dominant triad are G-B-D. This is what happens when extra notes are added to this triad, a third higher every time:

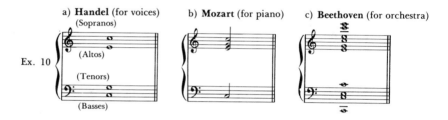

Ex. 11

V^7 (dominant 7th) V^9 (dominant 9th) V^{11} (dominant 11th) V^{13} (dominant 13th)

CONCORDS AND DISCORDS

A **concord** is a chord in which all the notes seem to 'agree' with each other. This kind of chord sounds 'at rest' and is complete in itself. In a **discord** certain notes 'disagree', or clash, creating an effect of restlessness or tension. Any discord sounds incomplete by itself – as if it needs to be followed by a concord in which the tension will be relaxed (or, as a musician would say, 'resolved'). All the chords in Example 11 are discords, and so are all augmented and diminished chords. There are other varieties of discord, found especially in 20th century music, in which the clash is even stronger.

Assignment 25

As you listen to the ten chords recorded on the cassette, note down whether you think each one is a concord or a discord.

12
Phrases and cadences

You will find that, in most cases, a composer shapes a melody by building it up in balanced **phrases**. A phrase is a group of notes which give a strong impression of 'belonging together'. The most usual length for a musical phrase is four bars, though phrases of eight bars, two bars, or just a single bar, are also quite common. Phrases consisting of three, five or seven bars are relatively rare.

A composer may clearly show how his melody is phrased by linking together notes within each phrase by means of a curved line. He may phrase his music in greater detail – for example, by using accents to indicate emphasis, slurs to imply *legato*, or dots to indicate *staccato*. Detailed phrasing such as this is used to tell string players how to use the bow, wind players how to 'tongue' the notes, and singers how to control the breath.

CADENCES

The ending of a phrase is marked by a **cadence** (from a Latin word meaning 'falling'). Cadences in a piece of music are 'resting-points' which serve as a kind of 'musical punctuation'. A cadence consists of the progression of two chords. There are four kinds of cadence:

PERFECT CADENCE (OR FULL-CLOSE)

The two chords which make up a perfect cadence are the dominant (V) (the chord built on the fifth note of the scale) and the tonic (I). A perfect cadence gives the music a sense of completion, of finality. Its effect is similar to that of a full-stop.

PLAGAL CADENCE

A plagal cadence consists of the subdominant (IV) followed by the tonic (I) and is another kind of musical full-stop. It is sometimes called an 'Amen' cadence as it is often used to harmonise this word at the end of hymns.

IMPERFECT CADENCE (OR HALF-CLOSE)

As its name suggests, an imperfect cadence makes the music at the point where it is used sound unfinished, incomplete. Its effect is that of a musical comma. An imperfect cadence consists of the progression of almost any chord – but frequently the tonic (I), the supertonic (II), or the subdominant (IV) – coming to rest on the dominant chord (V):

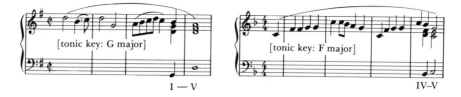

[tonic key: G major]   I — V

[tonic key: F major]   IV–V

INTERRUPTED CADENCE (OR 'SURPRISE' CADENCE)

This is quite easy to recognise since, as the name suggests, the music *sounds* interrupted. The composer leads us to expect a perfect cadence (V-I) – but instead of the dominant chord being followed by the expected tonic, the ear is surprised by a quite different chord instead. This is frequently the submediant (VI), as in the first example below. But the composer may use a more startling chord to heighten the 'surprise', as in the second example.

[tonic key: C major]   V(7)–VI

[tonic key: G major] *sfz*   V — !

TIERCE DE PICARDIE

Sometimes, the final cadence of a piece in a minor key ends with a major chord instead of the expected minor. This interesting effect (suggesting light after darkness) is known as a *tierce de Picardie*, or 'Picardy third' – referring to the major 3rd in the final chord.

[tonic key: D minor]

Assignment 26

Play or listen to this setting of the hymn-tune called *Old Hundredth*. Identify the cadences you hear.

Assignment 27

Sing or play other folk-tunes or hymn-tunes. Identify the cadence at the end of each phrase.

13
Modulation

Modulation is the change of key during a composition. In a short, simple piece there may be no modulation – the music stays in the same key throughout. But a longer piece would sound very dull without some change of key to add interest and variety. (The 20th century composer Arnold Schoenberg described modulation as 'a change of scenery'.)

Take for example a piece which begins and ends in C major. In this case, we call C major the *tonic key*. If the music modulates to the key of G major, we call this a modulation to the *dominant key* – the key a fifth higher than the tonic (see the diagram on page 12).

Of course, a composer may modulate to any key he chooses. But for whichever key he selects as his tonic (the main key, or 'home' key, in which the music begins and ends) there are a few other keys which are closely related. Modulation between these keys will sound particularly smooth and natural. Think of the tonic key of any piece as the *key-centre* around which these related keys revolve.

The three most closely related keys to any tonic, or key-centre, are:

the **dominant**: the key a fifth higher than the tonic, whose key signature contains either one sharp more or one flat less;

the **subdominant**: the key a fourth higher than the tonic, whose key signature contains either one flat more or one sharp less;

the **relative key**: if the tonic is a major key, the *relative minor* – the minor key sharing the same signature; if the tonic is a minor key, the *relative major* – the major key sharing the same signature. (See the chart of key signatures on page 13.)

The two charts below show these three most closely related keys – first, when the tonic is a *major* key (taking C major as an example); secondly, when the tonic is a *minor* key (with C minor as an example).

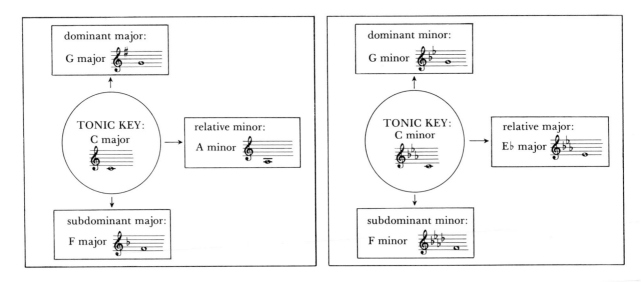

Assignment 28   Make diagrams similar to those above to show the three most closely related keys to (1) G major and G minor; (2) D major and D minor.

Special Assignment C

Here are four contrasted pieces of music. Carefully read through the questions set on each piece; then discover the answers by listening to the music and investigating the printed score.

1 **Romance from *Eine Kleine Nachtmusik***
('A Little Night Music')   Mozart (1756-1791)

1. Write Mozart's time signature in another way.

2. Explain these signs: :‖:   :‖

3. Draw, and name, three kinds of rest which Mozart uses in this music. For each rest, draw a note which has the same value.

4. Give the meaning of these dynamic markings which Mozart uses:
    p   *f*   *fp*

5. Which of these Italian terms should appear below bar 11?
    crescendo; diminuendo; ritenuto.

6. The following list includes Mozart's tempo marking, *andante*. Arrange the five words in order, slow to fast:
    andante; allegro; allegretto; adagio; andantino.

7. In which key does this Romance begin?

8. In bars 11 and 12 the music modulates to the dominant key. Which key is this?

9. The first 8 bars of this piece consist of two phrases of music. What kind of cadence ends the first phrase? Name the kind of cadence which ends the second phrase.

10. Which of the following note-values does *not* appear in bars 1 and 2 of this extract?
    (a) semiquaver; (b) quaver; (c) dotted quaver; (d) crotchet; (e) dotted crotchet; (e) minim.

11. Name the kind of interval formed between:
    (a) the first two notes of bar 7;
    (b) the first two notes of bar 9;
    (c) the first two notes of bar 13.

12. In which bar is there an appoggiatura? What is an appoggiatura?

2 **A movement from a Violin Sonata by an anonymous Baroque composer**

1. Which key does the composer choose as his tonic, or key-centre, for this piece?

2. By bar 4, the music has modulated to the relative major. Which key is this?

3. During bars 5 to 8, the music modulates again – to which key? (One of the two flats in the original key signature is cancelled, leaving a key whose signature has just one flat: B flat – but which also has C sharp as its *leading-note*.)

4. At the beginning of section B of this piece, the music modulates to the key of C minor. How is C minor related to the original tonic key?

5. At bars 12-14, the composer makes use of a special melodic device (marked by the square brackets). Is this device called sequence, imitation, or inversion?

6. With which kind of cadence does this music end? Is it: imperfect; perfect; plagal; or interrupted?

7. The first chord of bar 9 is built from a G major triad. How does the composer arrange the notes of this chord – is the chord in root position, first inversion, or second inversion?

8. Name the notes, and the kind of triad, from which the final chord is built. In which position is this chord arranged?

9. Which instruments play this Sonata?

10. Suggest a suitable Italian tempo marking which might be written at the beginning of this piece.

1. One of the figures is missing from the time signature. What figure should it be?

2. Which key does Haydn choose as his tonic key for this music?

3. At bars 12-14, the music modulates to the relative minor key. Which key is this?

4. At bars 14-20, the music modulates to another key (the accidental which appears is the leading-note of this new key). Which key is it? How is this key related to the tonic key?

5. Suggest a dynamic marking which might be written:
   (a) at the beginning of the piece;
   (b) at the end of bar 4;
   (c) at the end of bar 6.

6. The phrasing at bars 11-16 indicates that the music here should be played *legato*. What does *legato* mean?

7. Some of the notes during this piece have dots above or below them. Which Italian word would mean the same?

8. In which bars of this piece is there *imitation* between the first violin and the second violin?

9. The opening music reappears at the end of bar 24. Is it exactly the same as it was at first – or does Haydn make any important changes?

10. Name the kind of cadence which Haydn uses:
    (a) in bars 9-10;
    (b) at the end of the piece.

11. In which bars of the piece does Haydn write a *sequence*?

12. Haydn gives this music the title *Scherzando*. What does this mean? Which bars of the music particularly seem to fit this idea?

4   Dance of the Slave Girls (one of the   Borodin (1833-1887)
'Polovtsian Dances') from the opera *Prince Igor*

1. Borodin's tempo marking for this dance is *andantino*. Is this slightly faster, or slightly slower, than *andante*?

2. What is the tonic key of this music?

3. The instruments which Borodin chooses to play solos all come from the same section of the orchestra. Which section is it?

4. Which of these rhythms is heard over and over in the accompaniment?

   (a) ♫♩ ♫♩   (b) ♩♫♩♫   (c) ♫ ♫♫ ♪

   What name is given to a snatch of music which is constantly repeated like this?

5. At bar 23, Borodin wants the music to be 'soft, in a singing style, with expression'. How would he write this in Italian?

6. At which bar does the full orchestra play for the first time?

7. Name the single percussion instrument which is heard.

8. Which of these Italian terms should be printed below bar 40?
           crescendo;   *diminuendo*;   *accelerando*.

9. Explain these signs which appear in this melody-line score:

          3   ⌢   *8va - - ⌐*

10. Name two composers of the same nationality as Borodin.

PART TWO: THE SOUNDS OF MUSIC

14
Timbre, or tone-colour

oboe

trumpet

violin

Timbre is a word used to describe the characteristic sound-quality, or tone-colour, of an instrument or voice. It is by recognising *timbre* that we are able to tell the difference between, say, a trumpet, an oboe, and a violin – even if all three play exactly the same note.

Several factors account for the distinctive timbre of an instrument – including the materials from which it is made, the way it produces its sounds, and the way in which these sounds are made to resonate (for instance, the hollow wooden body of the violin). The most important factor, however, is to do with *harmonics*.

When a stretched string, or the air in a length of tube, is made to vibrate, it not only vibrates as a whole – but at the same time in two halves, three thirds, four quarters, and so on. The note sounded by the vibrations of the whole is the one we hear most strongly. But this main note is only the lowest, or *fundamental*, of a whole range of notes called the *harmonic series* (see page 45). The vibrations of the halves, thirds, and so on, are at the same time producing fainter, higher sounds, called *harmonics* or *overtones*. These 'colour' the tone of the main note.

Some instruments produce more harmonics than others. And different instruments emphasise different harmonics. It is, in fact, the relative strengths of the harmonics, and the way they mix together, which give an instrument its distinctive and characteristic timbre. They also help the determine the brilliance (or lack of brilliance) of its sound.

COMBINATIONS OF TIMBRES

A composer may smoothly blend together the timbres of certain instruments – for example: those of the same type, such as the string section of the orchestra; or perhaps instruments which share certain qualities of sound, such as the rich, dark tone-colours of violas, cellos, cor anglais and bassoons. Or he may choose to combine timbres which sharply contrast against each other to produce a colourful, clashing effect – for example: the brilliant, penetrating sounds of piccolo, high clarinets, muted trumpet and xylophone, perhaps against a more sombre background of horns, low woodwind and muted strings.

Assignment 29

Listen to the opening of each of these compositions. For each piece:
(i) identify the main sounds you hear, briefly describing the timbre of each one; (ii) describe how the various timbres are being combined (for instance: blended, or contrasted; or perhaps both – in turn).
(a) Samuel Barber: *Adagio*, Opus 11
(b) Handel: *Allegro deciso* from *The Water Music*
(c) Bruckner: second movement from Symphony No. 7 in E major
(d) Stravinsky: 'Infernal Dance of King Kastchei' from *The Firebird*
(e) Webern: No. 5 of *Five Pieces for Orchestra*, Opus 10

15
Texture

Some pieces of music present a rather dense sound: rich, and perhaps smoothly flowing. Other pieces may have a lighter, sparser sound, perhaps producing an effect which is angular or spiky. We call this aspect the **texture** of the music – likening the way in which the sounds are woven together in a musical composition to the way in which the threads are woven in a piece of fabric.

There are three main ways in which a composer may weave the 'fabric' of his music:

MONOPHONIC TEXTURE

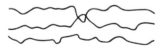

This is the simplest kind of musical texture. *Monophonic* texture consists of a single melodic line, without supporting harmonies – though the single melody may be performed by several voices and/or instruments, and perhaps accompanied by percussion instruments or a drone (one or two notes sounding continuously, usually in the bass).

Kinds of music which have a monophonic texture include the plainchants of the early Christian Church, medieval songs and dances, and much of the music belonging to Eastern cultures such as the Arab nations, India, China and Japan.

As an example of music which has a monophonic texture, listen to the beginning of the 9th century plainchant, *Veni Creator Spiritus*. (In medieval times, when this hymn was sung each Whitsunday, it was marked by a ceremony involving the use of incense, special vestments, lights, and the ringing of bells.)

Ve-ni Cre-a-tor Spi-ri-tus, Men-tes tu-o-rum vi-si-ta: Im-ple su-per-na gra-ti-a Quae tu cre-a-sti pec-to-ra.

POLYPHONIC, OR CONTRAPUNTAL, TEXTURE

In a *polyphonic*, or *contrapuntal*, texture (both words have the same meaning) two or more equally important melodic lines weave along at the same time. Quite different melodies may be combined together. Or the contrapuntal texture may be woven from just one musical idea with the voices or instruments entering successively in *imitation*. (If you have ever sung a canon or round, then you have taken part in a contrapuntal piece – perhaps without realising it!)

Listen to the opening of the slow movement of Bach's *Brandenburg Concerto No. 2*. Against a background supplied by harpsichord and cello, Bach weaves together three differently coloured strands of music – for violin, oboe, and recorder (in some performances replaced by flute). All three strands are fashioned from the same melodic idea:

(etc.)

HOMOPHONIC TEXTURE

Texture which is *homophonic* focusses attention upon a single melody. This kind of texture may be described as 'melody-plus-accompaniment'. The melody is usually (though not always) at the top of the texture.

Whereas in a polyphonic (or contrapuntal) texture each melodic line is of equal importance, in a homophonic texture a single melody claims importance while the other parts in the texture supply some kind of chordal accompaniment.

As an example of music which is homophonic in texture, listen to the beginning of Chopin's Prelude No. 4 in E minor:

The musical texture need not remain exactly the same right through a piece. For variety, a composer may decide to use homophonic and polyphonic textures in alternation. Listen to the 'Hallelujah Chorus' from *Messiah*, and you will find that much of the impact of the music is due to the way in which Handel varies the texture from one moment to the next in order to highlight the meaning of the words.

A composer may also vary texture in other ways – contrasting thick with thin, heavy with light, *legato* with *staccato*, and so on. The kind of rhythm used, and the ways in which different timbres are blended or contrasted, can also play an important part in creating a particular kind of texture.

Assignment 30

As you listen to the beginning of each of these pieces (not necessarily in the same order as printed here) describe in as much detail as you can the kind of texture which the music presents.

(a) Beethoven: the slow movement from Piano Concerto No. 5 in E flat (the 'Emperor')

(b) Bach: the final movement from *Brandenburg Concerto No. 2*

(c) A piece from India, China, Japan, or an Arab country

(d) Palestrina: *Missa Papae Marcelli* (Mass in memory of Pope Marcellus)

(e) Mozart: the second movement from Clarinet Concerto in A major

(f) A song by a Troubadour composer, such as *Kalenda Maya* (The First of May) by Raimbault de Vacqueiras

(g) Bartók: *Music for Strings, Percussion and Celesta*

(h) Stravinsky: 'Round Dance of the Princesses' from *The Firebird* (during the first one-and-a-quarter minutes or so of this piece, two kinds of texture are heard in alternation)

16
Contrasts

One of the most exciting effects a composer can create in his music is that of **contrast** – setting one kind of sound, or combination of sounds, against another. There may be contrast between the separate movements (or pieces) which make up a large composition; or between the various sections of music which make up a single piece; or even, in many pieces, contrast of some kind from one moment to the next.

The number of ways in which a composer may create contrast is countless – limited only by the extent of his musical imagination. Here are just a few:

---

pitch higher sounds contrasted against lower sounds

dynamics soft/loud

tempo (speed) quick/slow

mode major/minor

rhythm perhaps a gentle, flowing rhythm contrasted with a more energetic or 'spiky' rhythm

time or **metre** a change in the number of beats per bar (for example, from $\frac{3}{4}$ to $\frac{4}{4}$)

mood joyful/sorrowful; fiery/calm; lighthearted/solemn; and so on

harmony concords/discords

modulation a change (contrast) of key

forces few against many; perhaps solo against chorus or orchestra

timbre perhaps bright, penetrating tone-colours contrasted against those which are darker or richer

texture dense/thin; heavy/light; *legato/staccato*, and so on; perhaps homophonic/polyphonic

. . . and sometimes a contrast between **sound** and **silence**

Many of these ways of making contrast are very closely connected with each other, and you will often find that a really striking musical contrast is in fact a combination of several of these effects all taking place at once.

Assignment 31

Listen to some of the pieces mentioned below. Note down all the different kinds of contrast which you hear.

(a) Vivaldi: the first movement of 'Spring' from *The Four Seasons*
(b) Grieg: Norwegian Dance No. 2
(c) Prokofiev: 'Montagues and Capulets' from *Romeo and Juliet* (Suite 2)
(d) Bizet: Prélude to the opera *Carmen*
(e) Bach: Brandenburg Concerto No. 2 – the ending of the slow movement followed by the opening of the finale
(f) Stravinsky: *The Firebird* – the last moments of 'King Kastchei's Dance' followed by the beginning of the 'Berceuse'
(g) Carl Orff: 'In trutina' followed by 'Tempus est jocundum' from *Carmina Burana*
(h) A piece for two or more groups of voices and/or instruments by Giovanni Gabrieli
(i) A two to three minute extract from a modern work, such as *Kontakte* by Stockhausen, *Jeux Vénitiens* by Lutosławski, or *Threnody: To the Victims of Hiroshima* by Penderecki

17
Voices

When we sing, air expelled from the lungs causes the vocal cords (two strips of cartilage stretched across the larynx at the back of the throat) to vibrate like reeds, and so produce a note. To sing a higher note, we tighten the vocal cords; to sing a lower note, we slacken them. The various cavities of our throat, mouth, nose and head, serve as resonators to amplify and enrich the sounds.

TYPES OF VOICES

The following names are used to describe the range, and also the timbre, of different types of voices. For each voice, the average range is shown – trained soloists would be expected to exceed these limits. (Music for tenor voice is sometimes written in the treble clef, one octave higher than the actual sounds.)

Men's voices: Women's voices:

bass   baritone   tenor   countertenor   alto, or   mezzo-   soprano
                                                  contralto   soprano

A countertenor is an exceptionally high male voice with a strong, pure tone. It was popular in England during the 17th and 18th centuries, and has been revived during the 20th century.

A boy's voice before it 'breaks' (meaning that the vocal cords thicken, causing the pitch to become lower) is described as either a treble (high range) or alto (low). Girls' voices are similar in range, but have a rather gentler tone.

COMBINATIONS OF VOICES

Various groups of voices may be combined to form a chorus or choir. The most usual kind consists of 'mixed' voices – groups of sopranos, altos, tenors, and basses. A female choir includes two groups of sopranos and one or two groups of altos. A male voice choir may consist of men's voices only, or of boys' and men's voices mixed together – trebles, altos, tenors, and basses.

Solo voices may combine to sing a duet (for 2 voices), trio (3), quartet (4), quintet (5), sextet (6).

Assignment 32

As you listen to extracts from some of the following pieces, see if you can identify the type of voice or voices that you hear. (Some pieces are for one or more solo voices; some are for choir.)

(a)   Verdi: 'La donna è mobile' ('Woman is fickle') from *Rigoletto*

(b)   Mozart: The Queen of the Night's aria from *The Magic Flute*

(c)   Bach: 'Grief for sin' from the *St Matthew Passion*

(d)   Mozart: 'O Isis and Osiris' from Act II of *The Magic Flute*

(e)   Schubert: *Erlkönig* ('The Erlking')

(f)   Puccini: Love Duet from Act 1 of *Madame Butterfly*

(g)   Bizet: 'In the depths of the sacred temple' from *The Pearlfishers*

(h)   Handel: 'And with His stripes' from *Messiah*

(i)   A song by Mendelssohn such as *Greeting*, or *I would that my love*

(j)   A song by either Dowland or Purcell

(k)   Verdi: 'Fairest daughter of the graces' from Act III of *Rigoletto*

(l)   Britten: Kyrie from *Missa Brevis*

18
The orchestra

We use the word **orchestra** to describe a fairly large combination of instruments playing together as a group - though the exact number and type of instruments which are included may vary considerably from one musical work to another. The modern orchestra is sometimes called the 'symphony orchestra', meaning that it is able to play symphonies and similar orchestral works, such as overtures, suites and tone poems. These types of composition usually require an orchestra which includes four different **sections** or 'families' of instruments:

strings • woodwind • brass • percussion

The way in which these four sections are arranged on the concert platform is a practical one. Because of certain 'family likenesses' which they share, the instruments within each section are grouped together. The platform is usually terraced, and the four sections are positioned in such a way as to achieve a balance and blend of the various instrumental sounds and tone-colours.

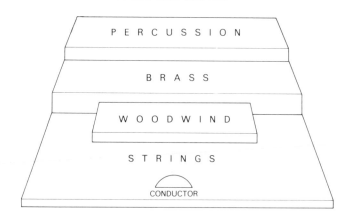

STRINGS

The strings form the 'backbone' of the orchestra - more than half the members of an orchestra play string instruments. The string section of a large orchestra may include:

16	first violins	10	cellos
14	second violins	8	double basses
12	violas	2	harps

Notice that the violins are divided into two groups: first violins and second violins. The difference is not in the instruments themselves (which are exactly the same of course) but in the music which they play - the first violins usually playing higher notes than the seconds.

Violins, violas, cellos, and double basses all produce their sounds in exactly the same way. Four strings - of gut, metal or nylon - are stretched across a hollow wooden body. They are fixed to the tailpiece at one end, then taken across the bridge to the tuning-pegs. Sometimes the player uses his fingertips to pluck the strings (called *pizzicato*) - but the more usual way of causing them to vibrate is by drawing a bow across them. This is a wooden stick with more than 200 strands of horsehair stretched tightly along it.

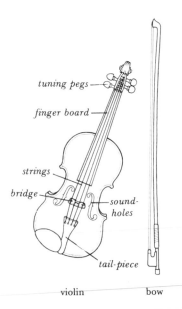

tuning pegs

finger board

strings

bridge

sound-holes

tail-piece

violin   bow

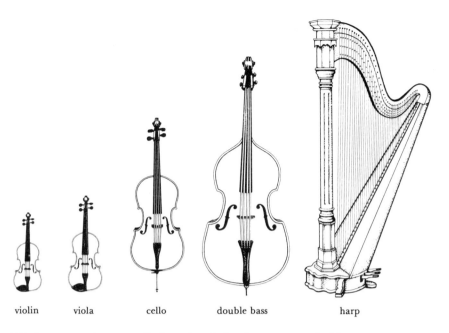

violin   viola   cello   double bass   harp

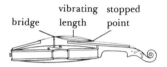

bridge   vibrating   stopped
length   point

We have seen (on page 4) that the pitch of a note sounded by a stretched string depends upon the length, thickness and tension of the string. The size of each instrument, of course, limits the length of its strings. The player cannot make them longer – but he can make different notes by *shortening* the strings. He does this by pressing them down to the fingerboard with the fingers of his left hand. This is called 'stopping' the strings. When a string is stopped in this way, only the length from the bridge to the stopped point will vibrate. The shorter the length of string, the higher the pitch of the note.

The instruments of the string section cover a wide range of pitch (see the chart on page 2) and can produce a rich variety of 'sound colours'. Here are some special effects composers sometimes ask for:

pizzicato plucking the strings with the fingertips; when the player
   is to use the bow again the composer writes the word *arco* (bow);
con sordino (with the mute) a comb-like device is clipped onto the
   bridge, damping the vibrations to give a hushed, silvery tone;
tremolo (trembling) an agitated, rather dramatic, quivering effect,
   usually consisting of quick repetitions of a note by making very
   rapid up-and-down movements of the bow;
col legno (with the wood) the player turns his bow over and uses the
   wooden part on the strings instead of the horsehair.

The harp

Although the harp is counted as a string instrument, its construction and the way in which it is played set it apart from the other members of the string section. The harp is always plucked. It has 47 strings and seven pedals, one for each note of the scale – a pedal for the A-strings, another for the B-strings, and so on. If a pedal is pressed down a notch, all the strings for those notes are slightly shortened and the notes sounded are a semitone higher. If the pedal is pressed down to the second notch, the pitch rises a further semitone.

Two typical harp 'effects' are *arpeggios* - spreading out the notes of a chord; and the *glissando* - sweeping the fingers across the strings.

43

WOODWIND

Although instruments of the woodwind section were originally made of wood, nowadays other materials may be used instead. The sounds are made by causing a column of air to vibrate inside a hollow tube. Along the length of each instrument there is a series of holes, controlled by a system of keys, springs and levers. By opening and closing these holes the player alters the length of the vibration column of air:

> the shorter the air column, the higher the note
> the longer the air column, the lower the note

double bassoon   bassoon

oboe   cor anglais   clarinet   bass clarinet   piccolo

flute

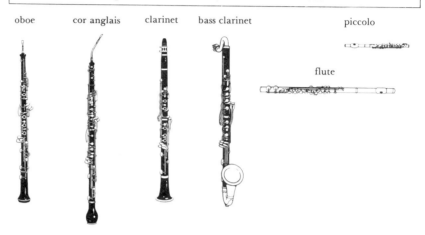

The woodwind section of the modern orchestra often includes:

2 flutes and piccolo	2 clarinets and bass clarinet
2 oboes and cor anglais	2 bassoons and double bassoon

Except for the flute and piccolo, each of these instruments has either a single or a double reed. The flute and piccolo – which are held horizontally rather than straight in front of the player – produce their sounds by what is called 'edge-tone'. The player directs a stream of air across an oval-shaped hole. The farther edge of this mouth-hole splits the stream of air and causes the air column inside the instrument to vibrate and so produce a note.

The clarinet has a single reed – a flat piece of cane shaved to delicate thinness at the end – which fits over an oblong hole in the mouthpiece. The player's breath causes the reed to vibrate, which in turn sets the air column vibrating inside the tube.

mouthpieces:

clarinet   oboe

The oboe, cor anglais (meaning 'English horn', but really a larger kind of oboe), bassoon and double bassoon each have a double reed – two strips of thin cane bound together, with the ends finely tapered. As the player blows, the two reeds vibrate against each other (in a similar way to the edges of a folded leaf, held between the thumbs and blown). The vibrations of the double reed set the air column vibrating inside the instrument.

Whereas the sounds of the string section blend together, those of the woodwind are more distinctive and individual, tending to contrast rather than blend. The woodwinds are frequently given solos to play, and so this section is placed in the centre of the orchestra, raised higher than the strings, and directly in front of the conductor.

BRASS Each instrument in the brass section is a length of hollow tubing with a mouthpiece at one end and a flaring 'bell' at the other. Although 'brass' is a convenient name for these instruments, they are more likely to be made of mixed metals nowadays than pure brass.

The brass section of the modern orchestra often includes:

4	horns
3	trumpets (and occasionally, cornets)
3	trombones (2 tenor; 1 bass or 'tenor-bass')
1	tuba

The pitch-range of each instrument depends upon its length of tube. For instance, the tube of the horn is longer than that of the trumpet, enabling it to sound lower notes (see the chart of ranges on page 2).

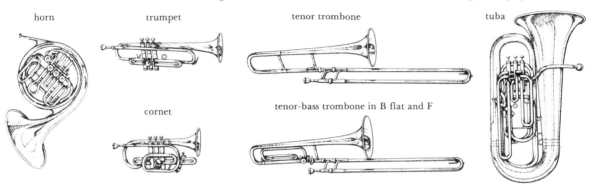

horn   trumpet   tenor trombone   tuba

cornet   tenor-bass trombone in B flat and F

To sound a note, a brass-player applies his lips to the cup-shaped mouthpiece and, as he blows, makes them vibrate – rather in the same way as the double reed in an oboe. This causes the air column inside the tube to vibrate also, and so produce a note. A player can sound several notes merely by altering the tension of his lips (tightening or slackening them – the tighter his lips, the higher the pitch of the note). We call these 'natural' sounds the *harmonic series*. The lowest note of the series, called the *fundamental*, depends upon the length of the tube. If a tube is of such a length that the fundamental is low C, then a brass-player, by gradually increasing the tension of his lips, might sound these notes (called *harmonics*, or *overtones*):

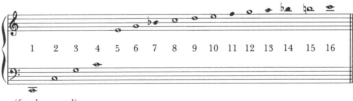

1 2 3 4 5 6 7 8 9 10 11 12 13 14 15 16

(fundamental)

However, on instruments of narrow 'bore' (that is, narrow tube-width) the fundamental is usually impossible to produce. There are several gaps in the series (those early on are particularly wide) and no notes falling within these gaps can be produced from that particular length of tube. Only the higher notes in the series occur close enough together to make any kind of tune possible – and even then, the black notes shown at 7, 11, 13 and 14 sound out of tune.

These were some of the difficulties faced by early trumpeters and horn-players. The main problem was limitation of available notes. To obtain more notes meant changing the tube-length of the instrument. Of course, trombone-players had always been able to do just that – to lengthen or shorten the instrument's tube-length by adjusting the 'slide'. Horn and trumpet-players, however, had to use a set of 'crooks' – extra lengths of tubing – any one of which could be fixed into the instrument temporarily to increase the overall length of the tube. But each crook still provided only those notes available from the harmonic series of the new total length of tube.

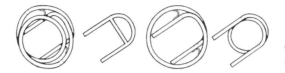

early 19th century horn, with crooks

The problem was finally solved around 1815 by the invention of the valve system. This is the same as having a complete set of crooks all permanently fixed into the instrument, any of which may be instantly selected by the touch of a finger. Each of the three valves brings in an extra length of tubing. When a valve is pressed down, the air is then diverted along the extra loop. Valves may be used singly, or in combination – offering a choice of seven different lengths of tube, each with its own harmonic series. (The length of tubing at valve 3 is in fact the same as the combined lengths of valves 1 and 2.)

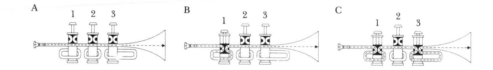

mouthpieces:

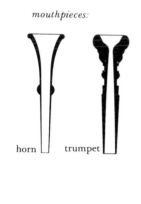

horn   trumpet

A player uses the valves as needed and, tensing his lips accordingly, selects the required note from the harmonic series offered. Notes from all seven harmonic series overlap, so making the instrument fully chromatic (able to play all semitones) throughout its range.

The tone-quality of a brass instrument depends upon the type of mouthpiece used, the 'bore' (or width) of the tubing, and the flare of the bell. The characteristic, brilliant sound of the trumpet, for instance, is due to its narrow, mainly cylindrical bore, the shallow cup-shaped mouthpiece, and moderately flaring bell. The horn, though, has a funnel-shaped mouthpiece and the bore gradually expands into a widely flaring bell, giving a rounder, more mellow sound.

The trombone is really a bass version of the trumpet; and the tuba, the largest and deepest-sounding member of the brass section, is in fact a large horn. The tuba was not invented until the 1820s, and so was provided with valves from the beginning.

Each brass instrument may be played with a *mute* – a cone of metal, wood or cardboard which is wedged into the bell. This alters the quality of sound, which may become thinner, muffled, as if coming from a distance; or, in *fortissimo* playing, rather metallic and menacing.

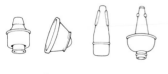

trumpet mutes

PERCUSSION

The percussion section includes those instruments which are struck or shaken, crashed or banged. These instruments can be divided into two groups. The first group contains *pitched*, or *tuned*, percussion – those instruments which can play one or more notes of definite pitch, and so could possibly play a tune. Included among these are:

kettle drums (or timpani)	glockenspiel (metal bars) xylophone (hard wood bars)	tubular bells celesta

The second group is larger and includes all *unpitched*, or *non-tuned*, percussion instruments – those which make sounds of indefinite pitch, and so can only play rhythms, not tunes. However colourful and exciting these instruments may sound, they must really be classed as 'noise-makers'. Included among these are:

bass drum snare drum (or side drum) cymbals	triangle tambourine castanets	woodblock whip (slapstick) tamtam (or gong)

Only on rare occasions will all these percussion instruments be heard in the same piece. In fact, some pieces (particularly those written during the 17th and 18th centuries) only make use of kettle drums. But many 19th- and 20th-century composers delight in exploring varied and colourful sounds drawn from a large percussion section.

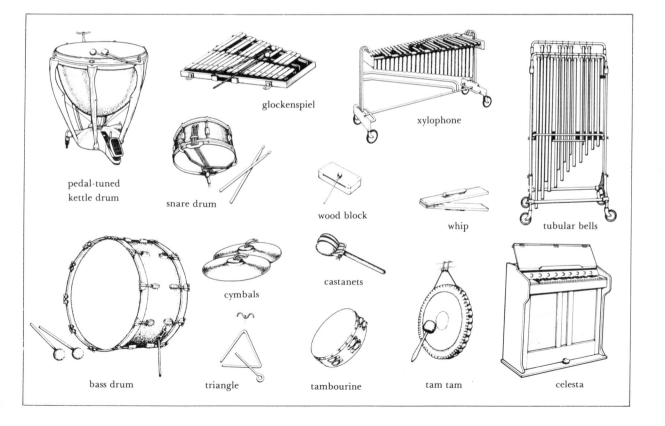

pedal-tuned kettle drum

glockenspiel

xylophone

snare drum

wood block

whip

tubular bells

cymbals

castanets

bass drum

triangle

tambourine

tam tam

celesta

Assignment 33   You will probably already be familiar with the sounds of the main orchestral instruments. If not, you will find it helpful to listen to Benjamin Britten's *The Young Person's Guide to the Orchestra* (also known as *Variations on a Theme of Purcell*) especially in a recording which includes spoken commentary.

First, Britten introduces the four orchestral sections; then he presents a series of variations, based on Purcell's tune, for each of the different types of instrument in turn.

Assignment 34   Identify the instruments which are illustrated in the box below. Give the name of the section of the orchestra to which each instrument belongs.

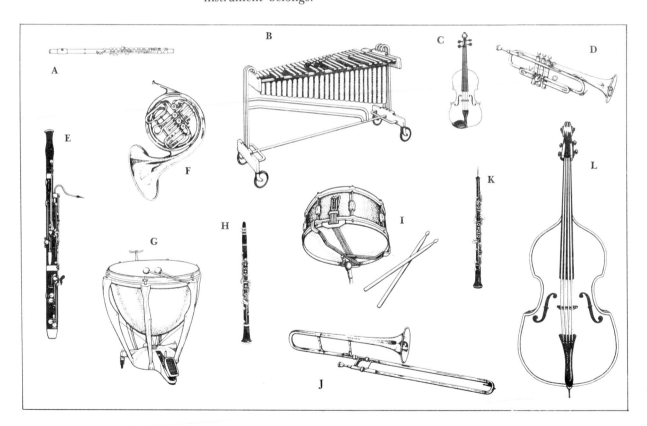

📼 **Assignment 35**   Identify each of the 15 instruments recorded on the cassette.

Assignment 36   Draw a chart similar to the one below. Then take each of the instruments you identified in Assignment 35 and enter its name in the appropriate box on your chart.

WOODWIND	BRASS	PERCUSSION	STRINGS
No reed	Valves	Pitched/tuned (notes)	Bowed
Single reed			
	Slide	Unpitched/non-tuned (noises)	Plucked
Double reed			

Assignment 37   See how many percussion instruments you can indentify in these pieces. Afterwards, make three lists, entering each instrument according to the vibrating material which produces its sounds: skin, metal, wood.

(a)   'Fandango Asturiano' from *Spanish Caprice* by Rimsky-Korsakov
(b)   Polka, from *The Age of Gold* by Shostakovich
(c)   Overture: *Tam O'Shanter* by Malcolm Arnold

Assignment 38   As you listen to the beginning of each of these pieces, identify the instrument which is featured solo:

(a)   Vaughan Williams: *The Lark Ascending*
(b)   Mendelssohn: 'Nocturne' from *A Midsummer Night's Dream*
(c)   Holst: *The Hymn of Jesus*; or the ballet *The Perfect Fool*
(d)   Bach: 'Badinerie' from Orchestral Suite No. 2 in B minor
(e)   Sibelius: Symphony No. 1 in E minor
(f)   Musorgsky: 'Bydlo' from *Pictures at an Exhibition*
(g)   Grieg: 'In the Hall of the Mountain King' from *Peer Gynt*
(h)   Bizet: 'La Garde Montante' from *Carmen*
(i)   Weber: *Invitation to the Dance* (orchestral version)
(j)   Delius: 'La Calinda', a wedding dance from the opera *Koanga*
(k)   Dvořák: *Largo* from Symphony No. 9 ('From the New World')
(l)   Arnold: No. 5 from *Eight English Dances*

19
How the orchestra grew

The grouping together of instruments of various kinds to form an orchestra first came about in the early 1600s. The first orchestras were haphazard collections of bowed and plucked strings and various types of wind instrument together with a keyboard instrument such as a harpsichord. Often, a composer would include whatever musicians were available to him at the time, and so the number of players and types of instrument would vary considerably from one composition to another.

Late 17th century to mid 18th century

Later in the 17th century, the development of the violin family led to the string section becoming established as a balanced and self-contained unit. This became a central 'nucleus' to which composers attached other instruments in ones and twos as occasion offered: flutes (or recorders), oboes, bassoon, perhaps horns, and occasionally trumpets and kettle drums. A constant feature at this time was the harpsichord *continuo* – the player 'continuing' throughout the music to fill out the harmonies and, in fact, to hold the ensemble together.

Late 18th century to early 19th century

Towards the end of the 18th century, the four main types of woodwind instrument (flute, oboe, the recently invented clarinet, and bassoon) were combined in pairs to form a self-contained woodwind section. The harpsichord continuo fell out of use, and instead a pair of horns helped considerably to bind together the texture of the music. Often, a pair of trumpets and a pair of kettle drums were included. For some time, this formation of the orchestra was accepted as standard. It is often called the 'Classical orchestra'; it is precisely this combination of instruments which is required to play Haydn's last symphonies, and the early symphonies of Beethoven and Schubert.

Mid 19th century

During the 19th century, both the size and range of the orchestra increased enormously. Trombones, which had earlier been used only in operas and church music, now found a regular place. The number of horns was increased to four, and the brass section was finally completed by the addition of the tuba. This section now took on far greater importance as its range and flexibility was increased by the invention of the valve system. Extra woodwind – piccolo, cor anglais, bass clarinet, and double bassoon – were available, and the choice of percussion instruments became more varied and excitingly colourful. It became necessary to increase the number of string players in order to keep a balance of sound between the four sections.

Late 19th century to the present day

At the end of the 19th century and the beginning of the 20th, the orchestra was, on occasion, vastly expanded – including extra brass, and triple or even quadruple woodwind. Around 1910, however, some composers began to write for much smaller orchestras: a small body of strings, one or two each of various kinds of woodwind and brass, and maybe one or two players controlling a varied selection of percussion. Some 20th-century composers have experimented with new sounds and new techniques: using newly-invented instruments; discovering entirely new sounds from familiar instruments; and sometimes exploring the exciting possibilities of transforming the sounds of the orchestra by using various electronic techniques.

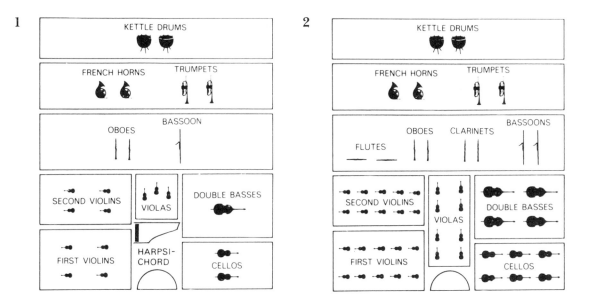

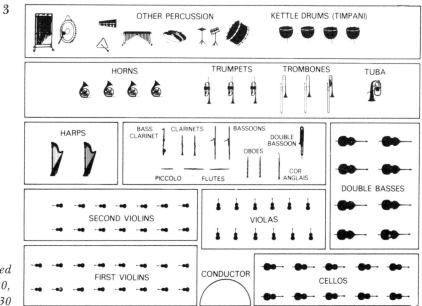

Three typical orchestras used by composers (1) around 1720, (2) around 1800, (3) after 1830

Assignment 39

Listen to extracts from some of the following pieces – but not necessarily in the order in which they are printed here. Judging by (i) the number of players, and (ii) the kind of sound or combination of instruments, suggest when each piece may have been composed.

(a) 'Alborada' from *Spanish Caprice* by Rimsky-Korsakov
(b) Mozart: Symphony No. 40 in G minor
(c) A movement from an orchestral suite by Bach or Handel
(d) Stockhausen: *Mixtur*
(e) A symphony by Mahler, or a symphonic poem by Richard Strauss
(f) Stravinsky: 'The Royal March' from *The Soldier's Tale*
(g) An instrumental piece from Monteverdi's opera, *Orfeo*

20
The orchestral score

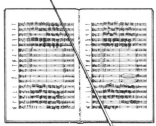

The music on this page shows the opening of the final movement of Tchaikovsky's Fourth Symphony. This is the first four bars of the music taken from the conductor's *orchestral score*.

The instruments are arranged down the page of an orchestral score according to the four sections of the orchestra. The order is always: woodwind, brass, percussion, and strings. If a harp is included, its music comes between the percussion and the strings. If voices are included, or an important solo instrument – for instance, in a violin or piano concerto (see page 70) – then these lines of music are placed immediately above the strings. (Sometimes, in older scores, the voice parts may be printed between the violas and cellos, so splitting the string section in two.)

SCORE AND PARTS

We can think of the full orchestral score used by the conductor as the 'master-plan' of the music, containing every note to be performed. The players themselves, however, read from *orchestral parts*, each player being given only that 'part' of the full score which he or she is to perform - as if all the pages of the full score were cut into separate strips and the lines of music arranged one beneath another on a page.

'TRANSPOSING' INSTRUMENTS

There are certain instruments which we call 'transposing' instruments. Their notes are *written* at a different pitch – higher, or lower – than they actually *sound* when they are played. There are certain reasons for this. Usually it is to make things more straightforward for the player; though there are other more complicated reasons which, though valid in the past, are now completely outdated.

The most straightforward kind of transposition is an 'octave transposition'. Look at the staves for piccolo and double bass on the orchestral score opposite. The piccolo notes sound an octave higher than they are written. The double bass notes sound an octave lower. In both cases, this is to save writing (and reading) too many leger lines above or below the stave.

The key of Tchaikovsky's music is F major. Although the piccolo and double bass notes are transposed to another octave, their music is still written in the *same key*. The music for other transposing instruments, however, may have to be written in another key entirely. For some (clarinets for example) the key signature is always shown. But for others (horns almost always, trumpets occasionally) no key signature is written. Instead, the accidentals (sharps, flats, and so on) are written in as they occur during the music.

(During the following, keep the note C firmly in mind!) The type of clarinets used in the score opposite are those built 'in B flat'. A clarinet in B flat *sounds* the note B flat when the note C is *written*. Its music must therefore be written out in a key one tone higher than it will actually sound. Another type of clarinet is that built 'in A'. The clarinet in A *sounds* the note A when the note C is *written*. So its music will be written a minor third higher than it sounds.

   Horns are usually 'in F'. They *sound* the note F when C is *written*, and so all their music is written a fifth higher than it will sound. Trumpets are often 'in B flat' in which case they behave exactly as clarinets in B flat - their music being written a tone higher than it sounds. However, in Tchaikovsky's score, trumpets in F are used. Written C will sound as F - but (unlike horns in F) the notes are written a fourth *lower* than they actually sound.

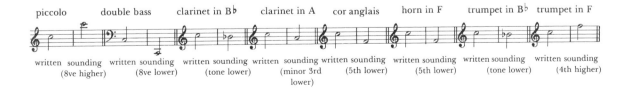

piccolo   double bass   clarinet in B♭   clarinet in A   cor anglais   horn in F   trumpet in B♭   trumpet in F

written sounding   written sounding   written sounding   written   sounding   written sounding   written sounding   written sounding   written sounding
(8ve higher)   (8ve lower)   (tone lower)   (minor 3rd lower)   (5th lower)   (5th lower)   (tone lower)   (4th higher)

FOREIGN NAMES FOR INSTRUMENTS

In most scores the instrument names are given in Italian, but sometimes other languages are used. The chart below includes all the main orchestral instruments. Except for percussion (for which there is no agreed order of instruments within the section itself) the instruments are listed here in 'score-order' – the order in which they would be arranged down a page of full score.

English	Italian	French	German
piccolo	flauto piccolo	petite flûte	kleine Flöte
flute	flauto	flûte	Flöte
oboe	oboe	hautbois	Hoboe
cor anglais	corno inglese	cor anglais	englisches Horn
clarinet	clarinetto	clarinette	Klarinette
bass clarinet	clarinetto basso	clarinette basse	Bassklarinette
bassoon	fagotto	basson	Fagott
double bassoon	contrafagotto	contrebasson	Kontrafagott
horn	corno	cor	Horn
trumpet	tromba	trompette	Trompete
trombone	trombone	trombone	Posaune
tuba	tuba	tuba	Tuba
kettle drums	timpani	timbales	Pauken
triangle	triangolo	triangle	Triangel
cymbals	piatti, cinelli	cymbales	Becken
bass drum	gran cassa	grosse caisse	grosse Trommel
snare (side) drum	tamburo militare	tambour militaire	kleine Trommel
tambourine	tamburo basco, tamburino	tambour de basque	Schellentrommel
tubular bells	campane, campanelle	cloches	Glocken
glockenspiel	campanette, campanelli	carillon	Glockenspiel
xylophone	silofono	xylophone	Xylophon
harp	arpa	harpe	Harfe
violin	violino	violon	Violine
viola	viola	alto	Bratsche
'cello	violoncello	violoncelle	Violoncell
double bass	contrabasso	contrebasse	Kontrabass

Assignment 40

(a) In which order are the sections of the orchestra arranged down the page of a full orchestral score?

(b) Whereabouts would you look for (i) music for harp; (ii) music for an important solo instrument (eg: in a piano or violin concerto); and (iii) vocal parts, when voices are taking part in the music?

Assignment 41

(a) Look at the orchestral score on page 52. Give the Italian name for each type of instrument taking part in the music.

(b) If you can, look at pages from scores in which the instruments are named in Italian, French or German. Give the English names.

Assignment 42

(a) Which orchestral instruments might use these different clefs?

(b) Which instruments would use no clef at all? Why?

Assignment 43 What is meant by 'transposing instruments'? Mention some examples.

Assignment 44

This score shows the beginning of the second movement of Dvořák's Symphony No. 9 in E minor ('From the New World'). Listen to these opening bars, then answer the questions below.

1. Note down the sections of the orchestra represented here. Then below each one, list the English names of the instruments included.

2. Explain: Largo. M.M. ♩ = 52.

3. Which instruments have *a 2* above their notes? What does this mean?

4. Explain: ——————   *dim.*   *ppp*   *con sordino*

5. The violas are marked *div.* (short for *divisi*). What does this mean? Name the first two notes these instruments play.

6. What do you think the slanting bars across the stem of the kettle drum's first note indicate to the player?

7. Clarinets 'in A' are used. Name the first note which they play:
   (i)   as it is written: (ii)   as it actually sounds.

8. Which other transposing instruments take part in this music?

9. Which solo instrument eventually introduces the melody? Write the notes it plays at the pitch they actually sound. (Include a clef, key signature, time signature, and dynamic marking.)

21
Bands

The name **band** may be given to any large combination of instrument-
alists, but it particularly refers to a group which consists mainly
of wind players – such as a brass band, or a military band.

BRASS BANDS

A **brass band** consists of brass instruments + percussion. A standard
brass band includes:

1 E flat soprano cornet
8 B flat cornets
1 B flat flügelhorn (treble saxhorn)
3 E flat saxhorns (tenor horns)
2 B flat saxhorns (baritone horns)
2 tenor trombones
1 bass trombone
2 B flat euphoniums (tenor tubas)
2 E flat bombardons (bass tubas)
2 B flat bombardons (contrabass tubas)
(Occasionally, saxophones are also included)

Percussion

The score of a piece of music written out for brass band looks
rather strange. All the instruments except the bass trombone and
percussion have their music written in the treble clef (even the
low-sounding bombardons), and are treated as transposing instruments
(see page 53).

MILITARY BANDS

A **military band** consists of woodwind + brass + percussion. The
number and kind of instruments vary from one military band to
another, but here is a fairly typical combination:

Flute and piccolo	4 horns in F or E flat
2 oboes	2 B flat cornets
4 (or as many as 16) B flat clarinets	2 B flat trumpets
2 E flat clarinets	2 tenor trombones
1 E flat alto saxophone	1 bass trombone
1 B flat tenor saxophone	1 euphonium
2 bassoons	2 bombardons
	Percussion

JAZZ BANDS

Jazz-players have always used the word 'band'. Early **jazz bands**
might be made up of about eight players – for example: cornet,
trombone, clarinet, saxophone, piano, banjo, string bass, drums.
Later, however, a group of this size became known as a 'combo', and
the name 'band', especially 'big band', came to mean a group of
15 or more players directed by a bandleader.

'Band' may also describe particular groups of instruments, such
as a steel band, percussion band, accordion band, and so on.

Assignment 45

Listen to varied extracts of music played by different types of band.
Identify each kind, naming types of instrument included.

22
Earlier instruments

In recent years, a very keen interest has been taken in what is now popularly called 'Early Music' – music written during Medieval times and the Renaissance (see the timechart on pages 94 and 95). A rich variety of instruments was used during these periods. Unfortunately, few of the original instruments have survived. But modern copies are made based on information found in poems and chronicles of the time, together with help from pictures in old manuscripts, paintings and woodcarvings, tapestries and stained-glass windows.

Here are brief descriptions of the instruments you are most likely to hear taking part in performances of 'Early Music'.

MEDIEVAL INSTRUMENTS

Medieval trumpet players

Pipe and tabor a pipe and a two-headed drum, played by one person.
Shawm a double-reed instrument (ancestor of the oboe) with an extremely brilliant, penetrating tone.
Organ besides the church organ there was also the portative organ, with few notes, and small enough to be carried as it was played.
Rebec a slender, pear-shaped bowed instrument with a rather 'reedy' tone; the number of strings varied between one and five.
Fiddle shaped like a figure of eight, and slightly larger than the modern viola; it had a flattish bridge, and usually five strings.
Hurdy-gurdy a wheel turned by a handle vibrated all the strings at once; sliders, pressed down by the fingers, could 'stop' strings at various points to give notes of different pitch.
Harp smaller than the modern harp, and with far fewer strings.
Psaltery the strings were plucked by quills held one in each hand.
Citole its four brass strings were plucked, usually with a quill.
Chime bells graded in size and pitch; struck with beaters.

Also: recorders of various sizes; the gentle Medieval flute; straight Medieval trumpet; long-necked lute (plucked); bagpipes; and percussion, such as cymbals, triangle, tambourine and various drums.

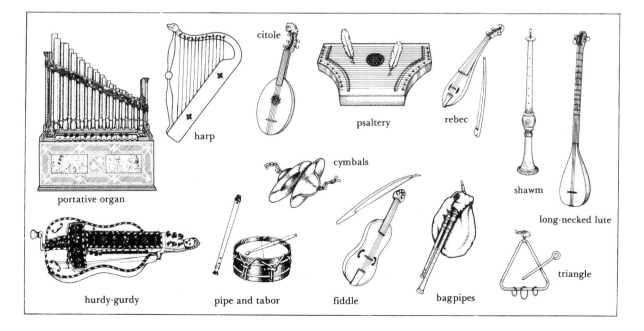

citole
psaltery
rebec
harp
cymbals
shawm
portative organ
long-necked lute
triangle
hurdy-gurdy
pipe and tabor
fiddle
bagpipes

During both the Medieval period and the Renaissance, instruments divided into two broad groups: *bas* ('low', or 'soft') instruments for music in the home; and *haut* ('high', or 'loud') instruments for music in churches, large halls, or in the open air. Some instruments, by the kind of sound they made, could belong to both these groups.

RENAISSANCE INSTRUMENTS

Queen Elizabeth playing a lute

Some of the instruments of Medieval times, such as recorders and shawms, still remained popular during the Renaissance. Others, like the lute, were altered and improved. And, of course, several new types of instrument were invented.

Many instruments, such as recorders, viols, shawms and crumhorns, were made in families – the same instrument in different sizes, so that there was a variety of pitch-ranges but a blending of timbre within each family. In England, a family of viols was known as a 'chest', since that was how these instruments were stored when not in use. Elizabethans called a group of instruments playing together a *consort* (similar in meaning to 'concert'). If instruments making up the consort were from one family only, it was called a *whole consort*; a *broken consort* consisted of a mixture of various instruments from different families – so that the sameness of the kind of sound was 'broken'.

Crumhorn   in this instrument, shaped like a walking-stick, a wooden cap enclosed a double reed, giving a rather soft but very reedy tone.

Rackett   a low-pitched double-reed instrument with a rather buzzing tone-quality. Nine parallel tubes were coiled inside a cylinder which was only a foot high.

Cornett   curved, made of wood or ivory and often bound with leather; with a trumpet-like mouthpiece, but finger-holes like a recorder. The tone could be varied from soft and mellow to extremely brilliant.

Sackbut   a name, popular in England, for the early kind of trombone. The bell was less flared, giving a rounder, more mellow tone.

Trumpet   the tube was now folded to make it more manageable; until the valve system was invented in the 19th century though, the limited notes available could be obtained only by varying lip-pressure.

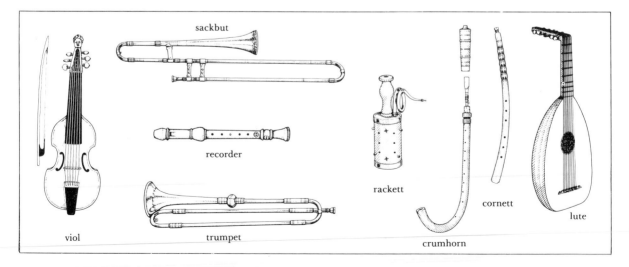

Woman playing a viol

Viols   the viol family was quite separate from the violin family which was just emerging. Viols had sloping shoulders and flat backs. There were six strings, and the fingerboard was fretted (like a guitar's) showing where to 'stop' the strings. The viol was held upright in front of the player rather than tucked under the chin. The tone was softer, more veiled and 'reedy' than that of the violin family. Chests of viols, consisting of three sizes (treble, tenor and bass – making a 'whole consort') were especially popular in Elizabethan England.

Lute   the plucked Renaissance lute was pear-shaped, with the pegbox bent back at an angle. The fingerboard was fretted, and the strings were tuned in pairs, called courses. The lute was used as a solo instrument, to accompany singers, or as a member of a consort.

Keyboard instruments   included the harpsichord, virginals, clavichord, positive organ and regal. In the harpsichord and virginals the strings were plucked. When a key was pressed down, a strip of wood called a 'jack' rose up inside and plucked the string with a plectrum made of quill or leather. Most harpsichords had a single manual (or keyboard) but occasionally double-manual harpsichords were made. These might have two or more complete sets of strings and jacks, brought into use by means of hand-stops or pedals, so that loud and soft sounds and different tone-qualities could be contrasted. The oblong virginals, popular in Elizabethan England, was a simple type of harpsichord with one string to each note, the strings running parallel to the keyboard.

In the clavichord the sounds were made by small brass blades called 'tangents' hitting the strings, then remaining there as long as keys were held down. Though the sound was extremely soft, the volume could be very slightly varied according to how firmly keys were depressed.

The positive organ was of medium size and able to be moved (positive meaning 'placed in position', on a table or the floor). Two 'players' were needed: one to work the bellows, one to press the keys. The regal was a portable reed organ, similar in tone to a consort of crumhorns.

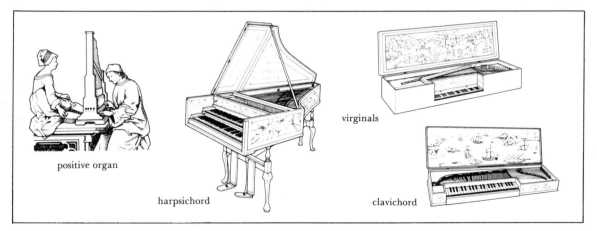

positive organ

harpsichord

virginals

clavichord

Assignment 46   Most records of 'Early Music' give details on their covers of which instruments they include. Listen to a variety of pieces, having found out which particular instruments take part in each item, and match their sounds to the descriptions and drawings on these pages.

23
The organ

The modern organ is the most complicated of all instruments. Its sounds are produced by wind blowing through several complete sets, or ranks, of pipes. In each rank the pipes are graded in size, and therefore in pitch, and each rank produces its own particular timbre, or tone-colour. Organs used to be blown by means of hand- or foot-operated bellows; but nowadays, in most organs, there is a blower powered by electricity.

The ranks of pipes are connected to two or more keyboards called *manuals* (from a Latin word meaning 'hands'). The *pedals* (from a Latin word meaning 'feet') are of wood and arranged in a similar pattern to the black and white keys on a keyboard. The organist plays on these by using the toe and heel of each foot. Notes are sounded by pressing down keys or pedals, so allowing wind to pass through the appropriate pipes. The pitch of a note depends mainly upon the length of the pipe:

> the shorter the pipe, the higher the note
> the longer the pipe, the lower the note

There are two main kinds of organ pipe: flue pipes, which produce their sounds in the same way as a recorder; and reed pipes, which have a thin strip of metal which vibrates as air passes through.

The organist decides which ranks of pipes will sound by pulling out various *stops*. Each stop controls a rank of pipes of a particular timbre. The sounds range from the basic and characteristic organ tone, called 'diapason', to sounds imitating other instruments, such as flute, trumpet, viola, and so on. The organist can mix together different kinds of sound, or he can contrast one against another, playing with each hand on a different manual. By using 'coupler stops' two or more manuals can be coupled together and played from one keyboard, providing a richer mixture of timbres and, when needed, a greater volume of sound.

24
The piano

The **pianoforte** – usually called the **piano** for short – was invented in 1698 by an Italian named Bartolomeo Cristofori. He called it *gravicembalo col piano e forte* – 'a harpsichord with soft and loud'. But whereas in a harpsichord the strings were plucked, in Cristofori's instrument they were struck by hammers – lightly, or more forcefully, according to the amount of pressure made by the player's fingers upon the keys.

This was to give the piano considerable powers of expression, and offer exciting possibilities. Not only might a pianist make sudden contrasts between soft and loud, he could also control all the various shades of tone and volume in between. Sounds could be made to grow gradually louder, or gradually softer, and further contrasts might be made between *legato* (smooth and sustained) and *staccato* (crisp and detached). A player might shape an expressive melody in *cantabile* ('singing') style with his right hand, against a quieter accompaniment with his left hand.

The modern piano has a range of up to seven-and-a-quarter octaves – greater than that of any other instrument except the organ. The strings of the piano are stretched across an iron frame. Behind this frame is a soundboard which increases the volume of the sound and enriches its tone-quality. Bass notes on the piano have a single string each, notes in the tenor range have two, and remaining notes have three strings each. The pitches of the various notes depend upon the length, the thickness, and the tension (or tightness) of the strings:

When a key on the piano is pressed down it sets in motion a very complicated mechanism which results in a felt-covered hammer hitting the string or strings belonging to that note. As soon as the key is released a felt-covered damper, lifted before the impact of the hammer, now falls back so that the strings are damped and their sound immediately silenced.

The piano has two pedals. The one on the right, called the sustaining pedal, causes all the dampers to be lifted, allowing any strings which are struck to vibrate freely until the pedal is released. If the pianist depresses the pedal on the left, called the soft pedal, a softer, more muted sound is produced. In an 'upright' piano this may be effected by a layer of felt coming between the hammers and the strings. In a 'grand' (horizontal, wing-shaped) piano, this pedal causes the entire action (keyboard and hammers) to shift slightly to the right, so that hammers can now strike only two of three strings, or a single string instead of two, thereby producing less volume (see the Italian terms *una corda* and *tre corde*, page 17).

Assignment 47   Listen to the three keyboard instruments recorded on the cassette.
(a)   Identify each one, and describe how its sounds are produced.
(b)   For each extract, suggest a likely composer, chosen from this list:
Monteverdi; Handel; Bach; Mozart; Chopin; Debussy; Bartók.

Assignment 48

keys	strings	pipes	pedals	hammers
stops	plectrums	tangents		

1.   Which of the words in the box above belong to each of these keyboard instruments?
   piano : organ : harpsichord : virginals : clavichord
2.   In which of these keyboard instruments are the strings plucked?
3.   In which are the strings hit?
4.   Which of them have pedals? What is the purpose of the pedals on each of these instruments?

Special Assignment D

1 'Scene' from the ballet *Swan Lake* Tchaikovsky (1840-1893)

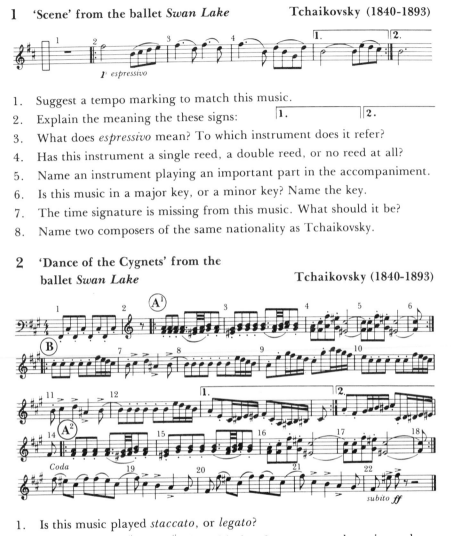

1. Suggest a tempo marking to match this music.
2. Explain the meaning the these signs: **1.** **2.**
3. What does *espressivo* mean? To which instrument does it refer?
4. Has this instrument a single reed, a double reed, or no reed at all?
5. Name an instrument playing an important part in the accompaniment.
6. Is this music in a major key, or a minor key? Name the key.
7. The time signature is missing from this music. What should it be?
8. Name two composers of the same nationality as Tchaikovsky.

2 'Dance of the Cygnets' from the
ballet *Swan Lake* Tchaikovsky (1840-1893)

1. Is this music played *staccato*, or *legato*?
2. The two notes F♯ and C♯ , heard in bar 1, are repeated continuously during section A of this music. Which instrument plays them? What name is given to a snatch of music persistently repeated like this?
3. Which pair of instruments first plays the tune of Section A?
4. This music is then repeated by two other pairs of instruments. Which are they? Which of these are 'transposing' instruments?
5. Which instruments take the tune in Section B?
6. The *coda* ('rounding-off section) ends *subito ff*. What does this mean?
7. In which bars of this dance is syncopation used?
8. Is this music in a major key, or a minor key? Name the key.
9. Section B modulates to the subdominant key. Which key is this?
10. What contrasts are there between music A and music B in this piece?

3 Pavane pour une Infante Défunte — Ravel (1875-1937)

Ravel originally composed this 'Pavan upon the death of a Spanish Princess' for piano solo, then later arranged it for orchestra.

1. Which instrument does Ravel choose to play the melody? To which section of the orchestra does it belong?

2. Which Italian word describes how the string instruments are played?

3. Suggest a dynamic marking for the beginning of this piece.

4. Which instrument plays the brief phrase at bars 6 and 7? And which instrument plays the phrase at bars 11 and 12?

5. On which beat of bar 7 does the harp play a *glissando*? What does this Italian word mean?

6. As a tempo marking, Ravel writes the French word *Lent*. Which Italian word would mean the same? What would it mean in English?

7. Explain: *rit. a tempo rall.*

8. Mention any other pieces by Ravel you have heard.

9. Name another composer who lived at the same time, and in the same country, as Ravel.

4 Second Movement from Symphony No. 7 in A major — Beethoven (1770-1827)

1. Which two sections of the orchestra play the opening chord?

2. Which instruments play the melody? To which section do they belong?

3. Give the letter-name of the first note of the melody they play.

4. Is *allegretto* a faster, or slower, tempo than *allegro*?

5. After the tempo marking Beethoven adds: ♩ = 76. What does this mean?

6. Is this music in a major key, or a minor key? Name the key.

7. By bar 10 it has modulated to the *relative* key. Which key is this?

8. Beethoven's dynamic markings have been omitted. He uses these four:

     pp   *p*   *f*   ═══════

   Suggest where each of these markings might be placed in the score.

9. Is this music homophonic, or polyphonic, in texture?

10. What kinds of musical contrast does Beethoven use in this extract?

11. Write out the first 8 bars of Beethoven's melody – first in the treble clef; then in the bass clef.

1. Which of following keyboard instruments plays this music?
    harpsichord;   clavichord;   positive organ.

2. How does the way this keyboard instrument makes its sound differ
    from the other two mentioned above?

3. In which bars of this Pavan (a slow, majestic dance) does Byrd make
    use of *imitation*?

4. Describe the kind of cadence Byrd uses to end the dance.

5. Name three other composers who lived at the same time, and in the
    same country, as Byrd.

6   La Coranto*   Thomas Morley (1557-1602)

1. Identify as many as you can of the instruments which play this lively
    Coranto (a 'running' dance).

2. Are they making up a 'whole consort', or a 'broken consort'?

3. What is the meaning of *da capo*, printed at the end of the music?

4. How many beats to each bar are there in this music?

5. In which bars does Morley use the melodic device called *sequence*?

6. The last line of music is basically the same as the line above –
    but Morley alters it slightly. Does he use *decoration, augmentation*, or
    diminution?

7. In which bars of this dance do you notice *syncopation*?

* Included on David Munrow's record, *Two Renaissance Dance Bands* (HQS 1249)

**7 Chorale: 'Herzliebster Jesu' ('O blessed Jesu')
from *Saint Matthew Passion***

Bach (1685-1750)

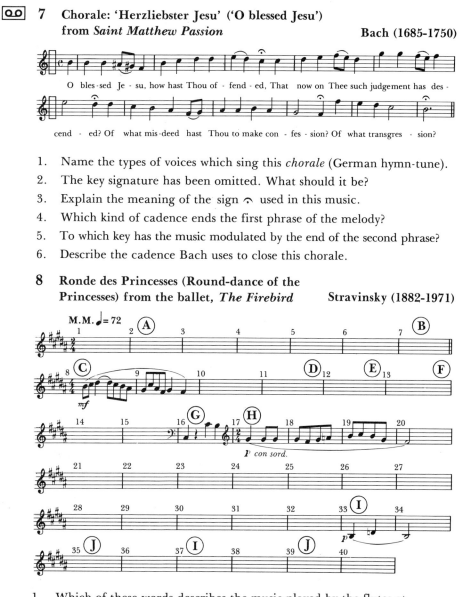

O bles-sed Je - su, how hast Thou of - fend - ed, That now on Thee such judgement has des -

cend - ed? Of what mis-deed hast Thou to make con - fes - sion? Of what transgres - sion?

1. Name the types of voices which sing this *chorale* (German hymn-tune).
2. The key signature has been omitted. What should it be?
3. Explain the meaning of the sign ⌢ used in this music.
4. Which kind of cadence ends the first phrase of the melody?
5. To which key has the music modulated by the end of the second phrase?
6. Describe the cadence Bach uses to close this chorale.

**8 Ronde des Princesses (Round-dance of the
Princesses) from the ballet, *The Firebird***

Stravinsky (1882-1971)

M.M. ♩ = 72

P con sord.

1. Which of these words describes the music played by the flutes at
   letter **A** in this score? *chorale*; *canon*; *ostinato*; *sequence.*
2. Which of these Italian phrases would be written at letter **B**?
   molto cresc.   *accelerando*   *poco ritard.*
3. Which instrument plays the melody at **C**? Which instrument accompanies?
4. At **D**, **E**, and **F**, solos are played by clarinet, bassoon, and cello –
   but in which order are these instruments heard?
5. Which Italian word would be written below the bass notes at letter **G**?
6. Name the instruments which play the melody at letter **H**.
7. This same four-bar phrase (letter **H**) is repeated later on. At which
   bars is it heard? Which instruments 'double' the melody here?
8. At letters **I** and **J**, two wind instruments play alternate phrases.
   Name these two instruments.

PART THREE: ALL KINDS OF MUSIC

25
Simple musical forms

We use the word **form** to describe the way a composer arranges and sets in order his musical ideas – the way he designs, shapes and builds up a composition. The two main ingredients he uses are *repetition* and *contrast*. Some repetition of ideas is necessary to bind the music together – to bring unity to the composition. Contrasts of various kinds (see page 40) are introduced to achieve interest and variety.

BINARY FORM

A piece designed in *binary* form is built up in *two* sections – the first section (A) answered, and balanced, by the second (B). Each of these sections is usually marked with repeat signs:

| Section A | :‖: | Section B | :‖ |

B may be the same length as A, or it may be rather longer. In most binary pieces, the music modulates to a new key towards the end of A; then returns to the tonic key during B. A and B usually share the same musical ideas – the chief musical contrast being one of key.

Examples

The *Minuet* by Haydn (page 22), *Gavotte* by Corelli (page 23), the Violin Sonata movement (page 34), and Byrd's *Pavan* (page 64).

TERNARY FORM

A piece designed in *ternary* form is built up in *three* sections, A B A:

| A^1 statement | B contrast | A^2 repetition |

A^1 and A^2 use the same music. Music B presents a contrast to music A, and usually brings in a quite different tune. When music A returns as A^2 it may be exactly the same as when it was first heard, or the composer may decide to change it in some way to add more interest.

Examples

The music by Haydn (page 35), and Tchaikovsky's *Dance of the Cygnets* (page 62). Listen also to *Grieg's Norwegian Dance No. 2*, in which there are several striking contrasts between music A and music B:

66

RONDO FORM

In a *rondo*, the main theme (A) keeps 'coming round' with contrasting sections of music (B, C, and so on) heard in between. The contrasting sections are called episodes. Here is a plan of a rondo designed as A B A C A (though some rondos have three, or even more, episodes):

A^1 main theme	B 1st episode: a contrast	A^2 repetition of main theme	C 2nd episode: another contrast	A^3 repetition of main theme

When the main theme (A) returns, the composer may shorten or vary it in some way. He may join two sections smoothly together with a brief passage of music called a *link*, and round off the piece with a *coda*.

Examples

'Rondeau' from *The Fairy Queen* by Purcell; the third movement of Mozart's Horn Concerto No. 3; and the Prélude to Bizet's opera *Carmen*. Here is a snatch of each of the three tunes from this last piece. You will find that Bizet makes it very easy to recognise his main rondo theme (A) each time it comes round!

THEME AND VARIATIONS

This is one of the oldest of all musical forms. As a theme, the composer takes a fairly simple, easy-to-remember tune, often binary or ternary in design. He first presents this theme in a comparatively straightforward way. Then he builds up his music by repeating the theme as often as he likes, but each time varying it – disguising or altering it in different ways: perhaps by changing the harmony, mode (eg: major to minor), rhythm, tempo, instrumentation; or by using any or all of the melodic and rhythmic devices mentioned on pages 26 and 27.

Examples

The slow movement of Haydn's 'Emperor' String Quartet; and the variations on a Shaker tune from Copland's ballet *Appalachian Spring*.

The ground bass

This is a rather special type of variation writing in which the theme – or 'ground' – is repeated over and over in the bass, while above, the composer weaves a continuous texture of melody and harmonies. 'Dido's Lament' from Purcell's opera *Dido and Aeneas* is a fine example.

Assignment 49

Listen to two or three of these pieces. As you listen, decide which musical form each composer is using to build up his music.

(a) Tchaikovsky: 'Dance of the Flutes' from *The Nutcracker*
(b) Handel: 'La Réjouissance' from *Music for the Royal Fireworks*
(c) Bizet: Prélude to *L'Arlésienne*
(d) Beethoven: slow movement from Piano Sonata No. 8 ('Pathétique')
(e) Schubert: fourth movement from the 'Trout' Quintet
(f) Järnefelt: *Praeludium* for small orchestra
(g) Prokofiev: 'Masks' from the ballet *Romeo and Juliet*

26
Larger forms

The musical forms described on pages 66 and 67 may be used as designs for separate, self-contained pieces of music; or they may be used to design one or more of the 'movements', the individual pieces, which make up larger musical forms such as the suite, sonata, symphony, concerto and string quartet.

SUITE

Allemande

(Bach: *Fifth French Suite*)

A **suite** (meaning 'followed') is a collection of pieces, often dances, grouped together to form a complete work. During the Baroque period (see the timechart on page 94) a great many suites were written for harpsichord, and eventually the most common plan brought together four dances from different countries:

(1) a German *allemande*: $\frac{4}{4}$ time, rather moderate in speed.

(2) either a French *courante*: $\frac{3}{2}$ or $\frac{6}{4}$ time, moderately fast; or an Italian *corrente*: $\frac{3}{4}$ or $\frac{3}{8}$ time, rather quicker.

(3) a Spanish *sarabande*: slow, triple time – often with an emphasis on the second beat of the bar.

(4) a lively *gigue* (English 'jig') usually in compound time.

All these dances were usually designed in *binary form* (see page 66). Sometimes a suite began with a *prelude* ('opening piece'), and before or after the gigue the composer might introduce one or more extra dances of French origin (called 'galanteries'). The most common were: the *minuet*: $\frac{3}{4}$ time, stately in character and moderate in speed; the *gavotte*: dignified, but often faster than the minuet, $\frac{2}{2}$ or $\frac{4}{4}$ time, usually with each phrase beginning halfway through a bar; the *bourrée*: a fast dance in $\frac{2}{2}$ time (occasionally $\frac{4}{4}$) with each phrase beginning on the last quarter of the bar.

During the 19th century it became popular for a composer to make an orchestral suite by collecting together several of the pieces he had composed for a ballet or an opera: for example, Tchaikovsky's suite from *The Nutcracker*, or Bizet's suite from *Carmen*. A similar suite might consist of pieces of incidental music written to accompany the performance of a play – such as Grieg's music for Ibsen's *Peer Gynt*, or Mendelssohn's music for Shakespeare's *A Midsummer Night's Dream*.

SONATA

Adagio

Violino I
Violino II
Violone e Cembalo

(Corelli: *Trio Sonata, Opus 2 No. 4*)

Sonata really means 'sounded', and therefore a piece to be played (as opposed to a *cantata*, a piece to be sung). During the Baroque period, many sonatas were written for two melody instruments (often violins) with *continuo* accompaniment. The continuo part consisted of a bass-line to be played by an instrument such as a cello. But the composer expected another continuo player on harpsichord or organ to fill in the harmonies by building up chords on this bass-line. Very often, composers supplied figures beneath the bass-line to provide clues to the harmonies which were expected. A sonata of this kind was called a **trio sonata** – 'trio' meaning three, and referring to the three lines of printed music, though in fact *four* players were needed. Sometimes sonatas were written for a single melody instrument with continuo (see page 34, where the small-sized notes show the harmonies which the harpsichord-player would be expected to provide). Baroque sonatas commonly consisted of four movements, contrasted in speed (slow : fast : slow : fast). Most movements were in binary form.

(Brahms: *Violin Sonata No. 1*)

From the middle of the 18th century onwards, **sonata** became the name a composer gave a work in several movements for one or two instruments only – for instance, piano; or violin and piano. If three instruments took part he called his work a *trio*; if there were four he called it a *quartet* – for example: a string quartet, for two violins, viola and cello (see page 71). A **symphony** (meaning a 'sounding together') is really a sonata for orchestra.

Most symphonies and string quartets, and many sonatas, are designed in four movements, well contrasted in speed and character, and usually set out as follows:

First movement

This is usually fairly brisk in speed, and almost always designed in what is called *sonata form*. This name is rather misleading since it does not refer to the structure of a complete work, but to a special type of musical form used to build up a single movement of a work – including symphonies, string quartets, and so on, as well as sonatas.

Sonata form actually grew out of binary (two-part) form – yet it is ternary (three-part) in outline in that it consists of three main sections, called **exposition**, **development**, and **recapitulation**. (There may be a slow introduction before the sonata form really begins.)

Exposition (presentation)			Development (discussion)	Recapitulation (restatement)			Coda
First subject (tonic)	Bridge (changing key)	Second subject (in a new key)	– moving through new keys, discussing, developing, combining and opposing ideas from the exposition	First subject (tonic)	Bridge (now altered)	Second subject (*tonic*)	to round off

(Beethoven: *Fifth Symphony*)

1. *Exposition* Here, the composer 'exposes', or presents, his musical material. He calls his main ideas *subjects* (meaning 'subjects for later discussion'). There are two subjects – each of which may be made up of several musical ideas rather than a single melody. These two subjects are contrasted in key, and usually also in character. The first subject is in the tonic key. Then follows a bridge passage which modulates, leading into the second subject in a new key.

2. *Development* In this section the composer 'develops' or explores the musical possibilities of any of the ideas he has presented in the exposition section. A strong feeling of tension, of dramatic conflict, may be built up, reaching a climax when the music purposefully makes for 'home' – the tonic key – and the beginning of the recapitulation.

3. *Recapitulation* The composer now 'recapitulates', or repeats in a slightly different way, the music of the exposition section. The first subject is heard in the tonic key as before. The bridge passage is altered so that the second subject *also* now appears in the tonic.

The composer then rounds off the movement with a *coda*.

Second movement

The second movement is slower in tempo, and more song-like. It is often designed in ternary form, or theme and variations; or perhaps 'modified' sonata form – that is, with no development section.

Third Movement

At this point, Haydn and Mozart wrote a Minuet and Trio. Beethoven transformed this into the brisker, more vigorous Scherzo and Trio (*scherzo* meaning 'joke') while keeping to the same basic plan. The overall design of this kind of movement is ternary – but each of the sections is a complete binary or ternary form in miniature:

A¹ Minuet	B Trio (a contrast)	A² Minuet
‖: a :‖: b(a) :‖	‖: c :‖: d(c) :‖	‖ a ‖ b(a) ‖

Finale

The final movement – often swift, and light-hearted in mood – may be rondo form, sonata form, or a mixture of both; sometimes, variations.

CONCERTO

One of the most exciting types of composition is the **concerto** (a word which may come from Italian, meaning 'get together'; or from Latin, meaning 'dispute'). The basic idea can be traced back to Renaissance composers, such as Gabrieli, who wrote pieces for two (or more) contrasted groups. This idea of opposition and strong contrast later led to the Baroque **concerto grosso**, in which composers contrasted a small group of soloists (often two violins and a cello) called the *concertino*, against a string orchestra which was called either the *ripieno* ('filling') or *tutti* ('all', 'everyone'). Harpsichord or organ *continuo* (see page 68) filled out the texture when the ripieno group was playing, and continued to provide supporting harmonies on those occasions when the concertino instruments played on their own.

(Handel: *Concerto Grosso No. 8*)

From the concerto grosso grew the **solo concerto**, featuring a single instrument in competition with an orchestra. The idea of contrast became stronger still, and the composer often gave the soloist some brilliant and very difficult passages to play.

The quicker movements of a Baroque concerto were often in *ritornello* form (*ritornello* = 'return'). This consisted of alternating tutti and solo sections – the tutti sections based on a recurring main theme:

| Tutti 1 | Solo 1 | Tutti 2 | Solo 2 | Tutti 3 | (and so on)

During the Classical period, the three movements of a concerto (fairly fast : slow : fast) corresponded to the movements of a symphony – but without the minuet. The first movement, however, was in a special kind of sonata form, beginning with a 'double exposition' section: one exposition for the orchestra alone, presenting the main themes; then a second exposition, with the soloist joining in. And there was usually one or more occasions when the orchestra paused and the soloist played a *cadenza* – a showy passage, based on themes heard earlier, which displayed the player's technical brilliance.

(Grieg: *Piano Concerto*)

During the Romantic period several changes were made to the concerto. Composers used a much larger orchestra, and made their solo parts increasingly more difficult. There was a single exposition – usually with the soloist entering immediately, then sharing the themes with the orchestra. The idea of polite competition found in Classical concertos was transformed into an exciting and dramatic conflict – the single soloist opposed to the weight and power of a large orchestra.

CHAMBER MUSIC

Chamber music is music written for a small group of solo musicians, and intended to be played in a room, or chamber, rather than a large hall. Whatever combination of instruments may be involved there is only one player per part, whereas in orchestral music several players may be sharing the same part.

Here are some of the more usual combinations of instruments composers use in chamber works. Each name (trio, quartet, and so on) describes not only the group of players, but also the composition they perform:

(Haydn: 'Emperor' String Quartet)

Trio (three)	*string trio*: violin, viola, cello
	piano trio: piano, violin, cello
Quartet (four)	*string quartet*: 2 violins, viola, cello
	piano quartet: piano + string trio
Quintet (five)	*string quintet*: an extra viola, cello, or perhaps double bass added to the normal string quartet
	piano quintet: usually, piano + string quartet (though Schubert's 'Trout' Quintet is for piano, violin, viola, cello, double bass)
	wind quintet: flute, oboe, clarinet, bassoon, horn
Sextet (six)	*string sextet*: usually 2 violins, 2 violas, 2 cellos

The larger the number of instruments, the wider the choice becomes – and it is usually impossible to tell from the title alone which types are in fact included. Beethoven's *Septet* (seven) is for clarinet, bassoon, horn, violin, viola, cello, double bass; while the *Septet* by Saint-Saëns includes piano, trumpet, 2 violins, viola, cello, double bass. Mendelssohn's *Octet* (eight) is for 4 violins, 2 violas, 2 cellos; whereas Schubert's *Octet* includes clarinet, bassoon, horn, 2 violins, viola, cello and double bass.

Assignment 50

Listen to extracts from a variety of chamber works from different composers. As you listen to each piece:
(a) note down the instruments involved;
(b) name the type of composition/combination of instruments;
(c) if you can, name the period in the history of music when the music is likely to have been composed.

Assignment 51

Listen to extracts from some of the following works (but in an order different from the one printed here). As you listen to each extract, decide exactly which type of composition is being played.
(a) a dance from a keyboard suite by Purcell, Bach or Handel
(b) a movement from a trio sonata by a Baroque composer
(c) a movement from a sonata by a Classical or Romantic composer
(d) an extract from a concerto grosso by a Baroque composer
(e) an extract from a solo concerto
(f) a minuet from a symphony by a Classical composer
(g) part of a movement from a symphony by a Romantic composer
(h) an extract from a string quartet
(i) part of a chamber work involving more than four instruments

27
Operas and oratorios

Ha, ha, ha, ha! here's a fine place for a game of hide and seek!
Ah ah ah ah! que-sta è buo-na: or la-scia-la cer-car.

(Mozart: *Don Giovanni*)

An **opera** is a drama set to music, acted and sung by solo singers (and often a chorus) accompanied by an orchestra. In some operas there are sections of spoken dialogue; in others, every word is sung.

For the solo singers there are *arias* (Italian for 'songs') and there may be occasions when voices are heard swiftly pattering off words in passages called *recitative*. In a recitative there may not be much 'tune'; instead, the melodic line closely follows the rise and fall of speech, and the natural rhythm of the words. There are two kinds of recitative: *secco* ('dry') in which the voice may be supported by plain chords on a harpsichord, perhaps with a cello strengthening the bass-line; and *stromentato* or *accompagnato* ('accompanied'), used when the composer feels that the dramatic nature of the words needs to be heightened by an orchestral accompaniment of some kind.

Composers use recitative as a means of swiftly 'telling the story'; arias are more tuneful and flowing, often portraying the characters' thoughts and emotions as they are affected by events in the story.

Here are a few of the most important composers of opera:

Monteverdi (1567-1643)	Rossini (1792-1868)	Smetana (1824-1884)
Handel (1685-1759)	Donizetti (1797-1848)	Bizet (1838-1875)
Gluck (1714-1787)	Bellini (1801-1835)	Puccini (1858-1924)
Mozart (1756-1791)	Wagner (1813-1883)	R. Strauss (1864-1949)
Weber (1786-1826)	Verdi (1813-1901)	Britten (1913-1976)

Soprano — Hal- le-lu-jah, Hal le-lu-jah, Hal-le
Alto — Hal- le-lu-jah, Hal le-lu-jah, Hal-le
Tenor — Hal- le-lu-jah, Hal le-lu-jah, Hal-le
Bass — Hal- le-lu-jah, Hal le-lu-jah, Hal-le

Accomp.

(Handel: *Messiah*)

Oratorio was born at about the same time, and in the same country, as opera – towards the end of the 16th century in Italy. An oratorio is a setting of religious words for solo singers, chorus and orchestra. At first, oratorios were very similar to operas. They were made up of recitatives, arias and choruses, and acted out with scenery and costumes. In time, however, oratorios ceased to be acted and were given musical presentation only, in churches and concert halls rather than in theatres.

Of the many composers of oratorio, the most important are Handel (his finest include *Israel in Egypt*, *Samson*, and – the most popular of all oratorios – *Messiah*); Haydn (*The Creation* and *The Seasons*); Mendelssohn (*Elijah*); and Elgar (*The Dream of Gerontius*).

Bach composed a *'Christmas' Oratorio*, and also three settings of the **Passion** – a special type of oratorio telling the story of Christ's Crucifixion. Besides recitatives, arias and choruses, Bach includes settings of *chorales* (German hymn-tunes) which he places at key points to intensify the most solemn and deeply-moving moments of the story.

Similar to an oratorio, but on a smaller scale, is a **cantata** (Italian, meaning 'sung'). Bach composed more than 200 cantatas for soloists and chorus accompanied by orchestra and continuo. A Bach cantata often opens with a weighty chorus, continues with recitatives, arias and duets for the soloists, then closes with a chorale.

Assignment 52

Listen to extracts from operas, oratorios and cantatas. Decide whether each extract is an example of recitative, aria, chorus, or chorale.

28
More music for voices

(Full anthem: 'If ye love me', *by Tallis*)

(Palestrina: *Missa Papae Marcelli*)

(Wilbye: *Adieu, Sweet Amaryllis*)

(Schubert: 'Dream of Spring' from *Winter Journey*)

Motet: a short, sacred choral piece, usually contrapuntal in style and performed *a cappella* (that is, without instrumental accompaniment) and with words in Latin. (The earliest motets, by Medieval composers, might include secular words and were often written for two or three solo voices with the lowest part, called the tenor, played on an instrument.)

Anthem: a short, sacred choral piece sung during a Protestant church service (the counterpart of the motet, but sung in English not Latin). A *full anthem* is sung by the choir throughout, usually unaccompanied. In a *verse anthem*, verses sung by one or more soloists with instrumental accompaniment alternate with sections where the whole choir joins in.

Mass: the most solemn service of the Catholic Church. The words are in Latin and usually sung in plainsong. But many composers have made choral settings, with or without orchestral accompaniment, of the five sections known as the Ordinary of the Mass – meaning those parts which are 'ordinary' ('unchanging') and so remain the same for each day of the church year. The five sections of the Ordinary of the Mass are:

1. *Kyrie* (Lord have mercy, Christ have mercy)
2. *Gloria* (Glory to God in the highest)
3. *Credo* (I believe in one God)
4. *Sanctus* (Holy, holy, holy), *Osanna* (Hosanna) and *Benedictus* (Blessed is he who comes in the name of the Lord)
5. *Agnus Dei* (Lamb of God, who takest away the sins of the world)

Madrigal: a short, secular (non-sacred) piece in contrapuntal style with much use of imitation. Usually for four to six unaccompanied solo voices, and popular in 16th-century Italy and Elizabethan England. In England, besides the 'madrigal proper', there was also the *ballett*, lighter in style and mainly chordal, with dance-like rhythm and a 'fa-la-la' refrain; and the *ayre* (= air, or song). An ayre might be performed by solo voice accompanied by lute or other instruments (such as viols); or with all the parts sung by voices, with or without instrumental accompaniment.

Lied: German for 'song' (the plural is Lieder - 'songs') but used especially to describe songs, usually with piano accompaniment, by 19th-century German Romantic composers (in particular, Schubert, Schumann, Brahms, and Wolf). An important aspect of most Lieder is that the piano is far more than a mere 'prop' for the voice. Instead, voice and piano are brought together in equal partnership. A Lied may be composed in *strophic* style, in which the same music is basically repeated for each verse of the poem; or in the style which Germans call *durchkomponiert* ('through-composed') in which different music is composed to each verse throughout the song.

Assignment 53

Listen to various kinds of music for voices mentioned on these two pages. Identify each kind of piece, noting down any 'clues' you hear in the music. For example: solo voice(s) or choir; accompanied or unaccompanied (and the type of accompaniment); sacred or secular; the language in which the words are sung; and so on.

29
Programme music

Programme music is music which 'tells a story' or is in some way descriptive so that it conjures up images in the listener's mind. Renaissance and Baroque composers had sometimes written programme pieces, perhaps for voices or for harpsichord, with titles such as 'The Battle', 'The Hunt', 'Song of the Birds', and so on. It was during the 19th century, however, when Romantic composers were linking music more closely to painting and literature, that the idea of composing programme music became really important. Many 19th-century piano pieces and song accompaniments are programmatic in character, but it was in their orchestral music that Romantic composers were able to express their ideas most vividly. There are three main types of programme music for orchestra: the programme symphony, the concert overture, and the symphonic poem (sometimes called tone poem).

THE PROGRAMME SYMPHONY

Many 19th-century composers of **programme symphonies** used the same basic plan as Classical composers before them (see page 69) but, at the same time, drew inspiration for their musical ideas from a literary or pictorial background. This *programme* – the 'story-line' or descriptive idea behind the music – may be suggested by title alone: for example, Schumann's *'Spring' Symphony*, and Mendelssohn's *'Italian' Symphony*. Or a composer may write out his programme in the greatest detail – as did Berlioz when he was composing his *Symphonie Fantastique*.

Not all 19th-century symphonies are of the programme type; but in many, even when the composer makes no mention of a programme, the mood is often so intense that we feel the music must be directly based upon emotional or dramatic events which he has personally experienced.

THE CONCERT OVERTURE

'Overture', of course, was the name which had long been given to the orchestral piece played at the beginning of an opera. However, the 19th-century **concert overture** had no connections with opera; it was a one-movement programme piece for orchestra (often in sonata form) and simply intended for performance at a concert. Well-known concert overtures include Mendelssohn's sea-picture, *The Hebrides* (sometimes called 'Fingal's Cave'), Dvořák's *Carnival Overture*, Tchaikovsky's *1812* and *Romeo and Juliet*, and Elgar's *Cockaigne Overture*.

THE SYMPHONIC POEM, OR TONE POEM

The **symphonic poem**, sometimes called **tone poem**, was invented by the Hungarian composer, Liszt. Like the concert overture, it is a single-movement programme piece for orchestra, but is often more lengthy and freer in construction. Liszt composed 13 symphonic poems, including *Les Préludes* (based on a poem), *Hamlet* (based on Shakespeare's play) and *Orpheus* (based on a Greek legend). Other composers soon began to write symphonic poems, famous examples being *Vltava* by Smetana, *Danse Macabre* by Saint-Saëns, *The Sorcerer's Apprentice* by Dukas, *A Night on the Bare Mountain* by Musorgsky, *Till Eulenspiegel* by Richard Strauss, and *On Hearing the First Cuckoo in Spring* by Delius.

Assignment 54

Listen to an example of programme music (such as the tone poem *Vltava* by the Czech composer Smetana) having first found out in detail the 'programme' on which the composer bases his music.

As you listen, describe how the composer portrays in his music the different moods and/or events in the programme.

Special Assignment E

1 *Pastorale* from the 'Christmas' Concerto   Corelli (1653-1713)

Largo

1. Give the meaning of *Largo*.
2. How many beats to each bar are there in this music?
3. Which instruments make up the *concertino* group in this Concerto?
4. In which bar are the *concertino* instruments first heard playing alone?
5. In which bar does the *ripieno* group join in again?
6. Which instrument plays the *continuo* part?
7. Explain the meaning of *continuo*.
8. What name is given to this type of Baroque concerto?

2 Hornpipe   Purcell (1659-1695)

1. Which instrument plays this music?
2. Purcell's time signature simply indicates that there are three beats to each bar. What is each beat worth?
3. What is the tonic key of this piece?
4. In which key is the music at bar 5? How is this key related to the tonic key of the piece?
5. Suggest an Italian term to match the speed and mood of this music.
6. Give the bar numbers where you hear a sequence.
7. Is this piece designed in binary form, in ternary form, or rondo form?
8. What kind of a piece is a hornpipe?
9. This Hornpipe is from a larger work by Purcell. Is that work likely to be a suite, a symphony, or a concerto?
10. What nationality was Purcell?
11. Name another composition of his which you have heard.

Larghetto **from Clarinet Quintet in A major** Mozart (1756-1791)

(clarinet in A)

1. What is the meaning of *Larghetto*?
2. Suggest a dynamic marking for bar 1 of this music.
3. Has the clarinet a single reed, a double reed, or no reed at all?
4. How many players take part in this Clarinet Quintet?
5. Which instruments are included in addition to the clarinet?
6. Which of these instruments is not playing in steady quavers?
7. Mozart asks the higher-pitched instruments to play *con sordino*. What does this mean?
8. The clarinet is a 'transposing' instrument. Which two notes are actually *sounded* at the beginning of bar 1 when C followed by F are the *written* notes?

4   *Allegretto* **from Symphony No. 5**   Shostakovich (1906-1975)

1. The time signature is missing from the music above. What should it be?
2. Which instruments play the opening bars?
3. Name the instruments which play the rhythm in bars 11 and 12.
4. Which section of the orchestra is most important in bars 13 and 14?
5. Name the instrument which is left playing the tune at bar 15.
6. In which bars is the following rhythm heard?

7. In the last few bars of this extract Shostakovich 'spotlights' a pair of instruments of the same type. Which instruments are they?
8. Explain the 'dots' and 'arrowheads' above their final notes.
9. Which section of the orchestra is not heard during this extract?
10. Which of the following words best suits the style of this music?
     March;   Minuet;   Gavotte;   Scherzo.
11. Shostakovich composed 15 symphonies. What is a symphony?
12. Name two other composers of the same nationality as Shostakovich who also composed symphonies.

5   The Swan of Tuonela   Sibelius (1865-1957)

1. Explain the meaning of Sibelius's tempo marking for this music.
2. Except for the double basses, all the string parts are marked *divisi* and *con sordini*. What do these Italian terms mean?
3. Which instrument plays the melody at bar 5?
4. One solo string instrument is heard in bar 7, giving way to another in bar 8. Name both these instruments.
5. What kind of drum begins a 'roll' in bar 8?
6. Mention some of the musical contrasts Sibelius uses in this music.
7. Sibelius's music portrays a black swan gliding upon the dark river which surrounds Tuonela – the realm of the dead in Finnish mythology. What name is given to music like this, which is descriptive and so conjures up pictures in the mind of the listener?
8. Which of the following describes this composition by Sibelius?
   sonata;   symphony;   concerto;   tone poem;   oratorio.

6   Chorus: 'And the Glory of the Lord' from *Messiah*   Handel (1685-1750)

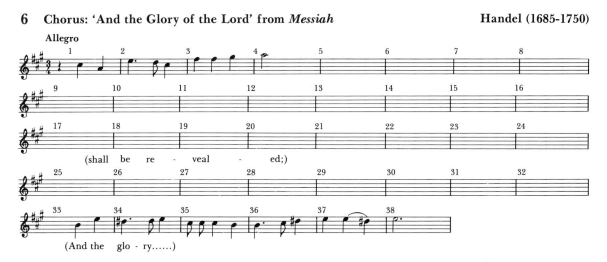

1. Name the four types of voices of the choir which sings this chorus.
2. Which group of voices enters first? In which bar do they begin to sing?
3. In which bar do the remaining groups of voices enter?
4. Is the texture at this point monophonic, homophonic, or polyphonic?
5. Which group of voices first sings the words: 'shall be revealed'?
6. Here, Handel introduces a change in musical texture. What kind of texture does he present at this point?
7. Does the texture of the music then remain the same until the end of the extract – or does it change once more?
8. *Messiah* is Handel's most famous oratorio. What is an oratorio?

7 'Che gelida manina' from Act 1 of *La Bohème*   Puccini (1858-1924)

How cold your lit-tle hand is! Let me warm it in my own. Your key, don't mind it, It's far too dark to find it. A lit-tle la-ter the moon will be ri-sing, __ and ve-ry soon then, the light will be strong-er. So stay a lit-tle long-er, and we'll talk a while to-geth-er, so you may know my vo-ca-tion, my am-bi-tions. Won't you?

1. Name an instrument heard in the introductory bars to this piece.
2. Which type of voice is heard in this extract?
3. Give the letter-name of the highest note which is sung.
4. Is this extract an example of recitative, aria, or chorale?
5. Which accompanying instrument plays an important part in bars 12-15?
6. What nationality was Puccini?
7. Name two other composers of the same nationality who also wrote operas.

8 *Pavane 'La Bataille'* ('The Battle Pavan')   Tylman Susato

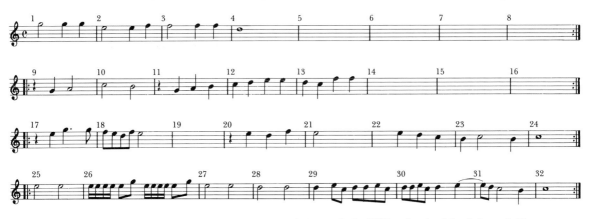

1. Write out bars 1-8 of the melody (filling in the blank bars 5-8).
2. Write down the three missing bars of melody at bars 14-16.
3. Name the instruments which play bars 17-18. Which instruments 'reply'?
4. Name, and draw, the three rests missing in bars 19, 21, and 22.
5. Name any percussion instruments taking part in this music.
6. Write down the *ostinato* rhythm which is heard throughout this Pavan.
7. What kind of piece is a pavan?
8. Is this Pavan likely to have been composed during the Renaissance, the Baroque, or the Classical period?

9 *Praeludium* **for small orchestra**   Järnefelt (1869-1958)

1. Which instruments are heard in bars 1-3? In what way are they played?
2. What name is given to this kind of musical device – in which the same snatch of music is persistently repeated?
3. Name the first instrument to play the tune.
4. One bar later another sets off with the same tune. Is this musical device called syncopation, imitation, diminution, or sequence?
5. In which part of which bar does a bassoon begin to play the tune?
6. Which instrument sets off with the tune at the end of bar 11?
7. To which section of the orchestra do all these soloists belong?
8. Järnefelt was Finnish. Name another composer from Finland.

10 **Third Movement from the Concerto 'Spring' from *The Four Seasons***   Vivaldi (1678-1741)

DANZA PASTORALE

1. How many beats to a bar has this music? What note is used for the beat?
2. In which key does the music begin?
3. Suggest a dynamic marking for bar 1, and another for bar 4.
4. For which solo instrument does Vivaldi write this Concerto?
5. In which bar is this instrument first featured *solo*?
6. Which melodic device does Vivaldi use in bars 15 and 16?
7. In which bar does the opening music return? Above this bar, would Vivaldi write *solo*, or *tutti*?
8. The theme is presented here in the relative minor. Which key is this?
9. In which musical form is this quick movement from a Baroque concerto most likely to be – ritornello form; sonata form; or variations?
10. Vivaldi paints a musical picture of a shepherds' dance in Spring. What name is given to music like this, which is descriptive?

Special Assignment F

In this assignment no help is provided in the way of printed music,
nor details given of composers or titles of the various pieces.
Listen carefully to each extract of music, gathering information
and discovering answers to the questions printed below.

Extract 1

(a) Name the type of voice which sings this music.

(b) Which instrument accompanies the voice?

(c) This music is an extract from an opera. Which of the following
is most likely to be the composer?
Byrd; Mozart; Chopin; Verdi; Stravinsky.

(d) Which of the following words describes this type of piece?
recitative; aria; chorale.

Extract 2

(a) Choose an Italian word to match the tempo of this music:
largo; *andante*; *allegro*.

(b) Which of these time signatures best suits this piece?
$\mathbf{C}$ $\mathbf{¢}$ $\frac{3}{4}$ $\frac{6}{8}$

(c) Which instrument plays the tune in this piece?

(d) Which instruments accompany? What name is given to these instruments, and the part they play, in a composition of this type?

(e) During which of these periods in the history of music would this
piece have been composed?
Renaissance; Baroque; Classical; Romantic.

(f) This piece is the final movement of a work in four movements.
What name would be given to the composition as a whole?

Extract 3

(a) Does this music begin in a major key, or in a minor key?

(b) The first player to be heard is instructed to play *una corda*.
What does this mean?

(c) How many instruments take part in this music? Name each one.

(d) What name is given to a chamber work for this number of players?

(e) Choose an Italian phrase to match the speed and mood of the music:
adagio mesto; *andante pesante*; *allegro scherzando*.

(f) Towards the end of the extract, each instrument enters in turn
with the same phrase of music. What name is given to this musical
device? Give the order in which the instruments enter with this
phrase.

(g) Which of these composers is likely to have written this music?
Corelli; Haydn; Brahms; Debussy; Stockhausen.

oo Extract 4
    (a) Is this music performed by solo singers, or by a choir of voices?

    (b) Frequently, a snatch of tune is presented in one voice-part and then the same snatch is immediately taken up by another. What name is given to this musical device?

    (c) The composer vividly brings out the meaning of certain words (such as 'ascending', 'descending' and, later, 'running down'). What name describes this technique in a piece of this kind?

    (d) Which of the following describes this type of piece?
        chorale; anthem; madrigal; ayre; ballett.

oo Extract 5
    (a) Which type of voice sings this music?

    (b) The title of the song is: 'To the Lute'. How does the composer bring out this idea in the piano part?

    (c) Would you say that voice and piano are equally important in this music – or is one more important than the other?

    (d) Which of these words describes this type of song?
        Lied; recitative; aria; madrigal; motet; duet.

    (e) The poem the composer chooses has two verses. Is his song 'strophic', or 'through-composed'?

    (f) Suggest a likely composer. (He is considered by many people to be the finest of all song composers.)

oo Extract 6
    (a) Name the instrument which takes the tune in this extract.

    (b) Which instruments play the accompaniment? How are they played here?

    (c) During the second part, one of these instruments 'doubles' the tune one octave lower. Which instrument is this?

    (d) In which of these forms is this music designed?
        binary; ternary; variations; sonata form.

    (e) Is the texture of this music homophonic, or polyphonic?

    (f) This extract is the Trio section of a *Minuet and Trio*, the third movement from a four-movement composition. What name would be given to the work as a whole? (The name also describes the particular combination of instruments taking part.)

    (g) In a complete performance of this composition, what music would you expect to hear after this Trio section?

    (h) Which of these composers is likely to have written this music?
        Byrd; Bach; Mozart; Wagner; Sibelius; Bartók.

oo Extract 7
    (a) Suggest a tempo marking for this music.

    (b) Name the instruments taking part.

    (c) Which of these titles best suits this music?
        Sarabande; Gavotte; Minuet; Scherzo.
        Give reasons for your choice.

    (d) This is an extract from the third movement of a four-movement composition. What name would be given to the complete work?

    (e) The music was written in 1802. Suggest a likely composer.

Further Assignments

Assignment 55 Name, and explain, these musical signs and symbols:

(1) 𝄢 (2) *p* (3) 𝄪 (4) 𝄾 (5) 𝄂

(6) **C** (7) ♭ (8) ♮ (9) *ff* (10) ⅞

(11) *D.C.* (12) ∞ (13) ⌁ (14) ▬ (15) ➤

(16) *con 8* (17) ◠ (18) ♩ (19) *sf* (20) *fp*

(21) ◁ (22) 𝄼. (23) 𝄡 (24) *8va - - ⌐* (25) *Fine*

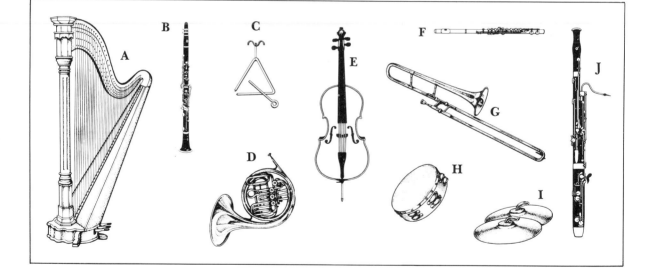

Assignment 56 (a) Listen to the 10 instruments recorded on the cassette. Identify each instrument, matching it to one of the drawings in this box:

(b) Name the section of the orchestra to which each instrument belongs.
(c) Describe how the sounds are made on each instrument.

Assignment 57 Name instruments whose music might include these Italian terms, telling the performer how the notes are to be played. (Some of the terms may apply to more than one instrument.)

pizzicato; una corda; arco; con sordino; glissando; Ped.

Assignment 58   Listen to extracts from the different kinds of music shown in the box below – but with the pieces played in a different order from the one printed here.

Minuet • Gavotte • March • Waltz • Polka • Tango

As you listen to each piece, note down:
(a)   the time signature of the music;
(b)   the kind of piece you are listening to;
(c)   whether the music is in a major key, or in a minor key.

Assignment 59   On a sheet of paper (turned sideways to give sufficient width) draw a chart consisting of seven columns, with these headings:

Piece No.	Melody	Rhythm	Insts/voices featured	Texture	Harmony	Mood
1.						
2.						

As you listen to recordings of different kinds of music, fill in your chart by writing one or two brief comments in each column to describe that particular aspect of the music.
Here are a few pointers to help you – but you may find that you can think of other, more suitable, words or phrases to describe the music.

Melody	Rhythm	Texture	Harmony
conjunct (moving mainly by step)	regular metre	monophonic (tune only)	concordant
disjunct (moving in wide leaps)	irregular metre	homophonic (chordal, or tune + accompaniment)	mainly concordant but spiced with discords
wide range, high to low	non-metrical	polyphonic/contrapuntal	very discordant
narrow range	syncopated	smooth, legato	calm, restful
clear-cut phrases	strongly accented	angular, spiky, staccato	tense, uneasy
lyrical, free-flowing	gently flowing	dense, heavy	many notes in each chord
wayward, unpredictable	ostinato used	thin, light, transparent	few notes in each chord
melody totally lacking			

Assignment 60   Listen to extracts from the different types of composition named in the boxes below. List the pieces in the order in which you hear them.

1	symphony	clarinet quintet
	violin sonata	
	piano concerto	string quartet

2	opera	oratorio
	madrigal ayre ballett	
	motet	anthem

Assignment 61   Listen to extracts of music performed by the various combinations of instruments mentioned in the box below (but with the extracts played in a different order from the one shown here).

	symphony orchestra	
string orchestra		string quartet
brass band	jazz band	
	military band	dance band

As you listen to each extract, note down which particular combination of instruments is playing.

Assignment 62   Listen to extracts of music composed during these different periods in the history of music:

Medieval (to 1450)	**Renaissance** (1450-1600)	**Baroque** (1600-1750)
Classical (1750-1810)	**Romantic** (1810-1910)	**'Modern'** (20th Century)

As you listen to each extract:
(a)   identify the period during which the music was composed;
(b)   name the type of composition being performed.

Assignment 63   Listen to extracts from pieces written for these different combinations of instruments:

cello and piano	2 violins, viola, cello
2 violins, cello, harpsichord	
violin, cello, piano	harpsichord and string orchestra

For each extract:
(a)   name the particular type of composition being performed;
(b)   identify the period during which it was composed (see the box for Assignment 62, above);
(c)   suggest a likely composer.

Assignment 64   Listen to film music of various kinds. For each extract, note down:
  (a)   A dynamic marking, a tempo marking and, if appropriate, an
          Italian term describing the style or mood of the music;
  (b)   A time signature;
  (c)   the kind of film for which the music was written, mentioning
          any 'clues' you hear in the music which suggest this (perhaps
          a special choice of instruments; a particular type of rhythm;
          certain harmonies – rich concords or harsh discords; and so on).

Assignment 65

This score shows the opening bars of a movement from a symphony.
 1.   Explain these terms and signs which appear in the score:
          a 2   *f*   *Allegretto* $\frac{3}{4}$
 2.   Look carefully down the left hand side of the score. Which sections
        of the orchestra are taking part?
 3.   For each section, name the instruments most likely to be involved.
 4.   Which instruments are playing the tune?
 5.   In which key is this music? (Take into account a key signature of
        two flats, with a leading-note of F sharp.)
 6.   Three of the top four staves in the score have the same key
        signature but the third stave has a different signature. This
        indicates that these instruments are transposing instruments.
          (a)   Which instruments are they likely to be?
          (b)   In which key is their music written? (Notice that there is
                  a leading-note of G sharp.)
          (c)   Write out their notes at the pitch they will actually sound.
 7.   Which other instruments in this score are transposing instruments?
 8.   Taking the time signature and the tempo marking as clues, which of
        the four movements of the Symphony is this likely to be?
 9.   Judging by the size and kind of orchestra, during which of these
        periods is the Symphony likely to have been composed?
          Classical;   Romantic;   20th Century.
10.   Suggest who the composer may be. (This is his Symphony No. 40.)

Assignment 66   Listen to the 10 extracts of music recorded on the cassette. For each extract, there are two questions.

1. (a)   Which instrument plays this music?
   (b)   Is it being played *con sordino*, or *senza sordino*?

2. (a)   Which of these Italian words matches the style of this music?
            alla marcia;   *cantabile*;   *scherzando*;   *agitato*.
   (b)   Is the composer Handel, Haydn, Beethoven, Debussy, or Schoenberg?

3. (a)   Which instrument is playing?
   (b)   Does it have a single reed, a double reed, or no reed at all?

4. (a)   Name the instruments playing this piece. What name is given to this combination of instruments – and also to the work they are playing?
   (b)   Suggest an Italian tempo marking to match this music.

5. (a)   Identify the instrument you hear.
   (b)   Would you class the sounds it is making as notes (regular vibrations) or as noises (irregular vibrations)?

6. (a)   Are these singers taking part in a madrigal, an oratorio, or an opera?
   (b)   During which century do you think this music was composed?

7. (a)   Which instrument plays this American folktune?
   (b)   Are the notes produced by means of pedals, keys, valves, or a slide?

8. (a)   What time signature would be written at the beginning of this piece?
   (b)   Which instrument plays this music? How are its sounds produced?

9. (a)   Which instrument is playing?
   (b)   Which of these Italian terms matches the sound?
            glissando;   *pizzicato*;   *con sordino*;   *arco*;   *col legno*.

10. (a)   The tonic note of this music is D. What will the key signature be?
    (b)   Name the composer (and, if you can, give the title) of this piece.

Assignment 67   In writing a piece of music, a composer is combining together several important musical 'ingredients'. These include:

melody • harmony • rhythm • timbre • texture

Listen to extracts from varied types of music, selected from the box below. Identify each kind of piece you hear, and note down which ingredients are most emphasised in the music.

a song from a 'musical'	a folksong	a plainchant	an 18th-century minuet
a German Lied	a piece of jazz	a 19th-century tone poem	a Medieval dance
a 20th-century piece involving electronic sounds	a chorale	a TV signature tune	a song from the 'Top 20'

1. Explain the signs ⌐**1.**ㄱ ⌐**2.**ㄱ

2. Identify as many as you can of the instruments which take part.

3. Which of these words describes the texture of this music?
   monophonic;   polyphonic;   homophonic.

4. During which of these periods do you think this music was composed?
   Medieval;   Renaissance;   Baroque;   Classical;   Romantic.

5. The piece is in four sections: A, B, C, D. In which of the following ways are these sections similar to one another?
   (a) all four sections are of the same length;
   (b) they all begin with the same tune;
   (c) they all use the same music for their endings;
   (d) they are all begun by the same solo instrument.

6. This music is an *estampie*. What kind of piece do you think this is?

Assignment 69

Taking the performance on the cassette as a guide, and using any available instruments which are suitable, try a group performance of *The Sixth Royal Estampie* (printed above).

Each of the four sections (A, B, C, D) is played twice – the first time with the 'open' ending, the second time with the 'closed' ending. Each section could begin with one or more different soloists; then everyone joins in for the 'open' and 'closed' phrases each time they come round.

Assignment 70   'Promenade' from *Pictures at an Exhibition*   Musorgsky (1839-1881)
(orchestrated by Ravel, 1875-1937)

1. How many beats are there in bar 1? And how many in bar 2?

2. Which instrument plays bars 1 and 2. Is it muted, or not muted?

3. Which section of the orchestra joins in at bar 3? Name four different instruments which are likely to be included here.

4. When is the instrument which played bars 1 and 2 next heard solo?

5. Name the section of the orchestra which joins in at bar 9.

6. Another section joins in at bar 10. Which section is this?

7. Which orchestral section is *not* heard during this music?

8. Why is no time signature shown for bar 9 or bar 10?

9. Musorgsky wrote *Pictures at an Exhibition* for piano solo. What does 'orchestrated by Ravel' mean?

10. Musorgsky was one of a group of composers who called themselves 'The Five'. Were these composers German, Russian, Czech, or French?

Assignment 71   'Pavane' from *Capriol Suite*   Warlock (1894-1930)

1. Which section of the orchestra plays this *Pavane*?

2. What is the tonic key for this music?

3. To which key has the music modulated by bar 11? How is this key related to the tonic key of the piece?

4. This *Pavane* is from a *suite* which the composer calls 'Capriol'. What is a *suite*?

5. Throughout this music, a single bar of rhythm is repeated over and over to imitate the original tabor-beat which accompanied this 16th-century dance. Write down this rhythm.

6. Write out the complete melody (bars 4-19), filling in the missing notes of any bars which have been left blank.

7. Write out the final four bars of the melody, one octave lower, in the bass clef.

8. Write out the first four bars of the melody, at the same pitch, but in the viola C clef.

Assignment 72   Listen to this piano piece:

1. Explain these Italian words: *Lento*;   *mesto*;   *legato*;   *Vivo*; *meno mosso*;   *Tempo primo*;   *molto rit.*
2. List the various kinds of contrast which are presented in this music.
3. In which of these musical forms is this piece designed?
   binary;   ternary;   rondo;   variations;   ground bass.
4. Draw a plan or diagram, clearly showing how the piece is built up. Using letters of the alphabet, label the sections of your diagram. Then use shading or colour to show sections of music which are similar, and any presenting contrast.

Assignment 73   Play or listen to each of these snatches of tune:

These snatches of tune form the beginnings of the sections of music which make up the *Gavotte* from Bach's Partita No. 3 in E major for unaccompanied violin. (This piece is sometimes heard in an arrangement for string orchestra, or in an arrangement for guitar by Segovia.)

Listen to the complete *Gavotte*, and discover which musical form Bach uses to build up his music by noting down the order in which these sections of music are heard. (One section is heard more than once.)

Afterwards, treat this piece in the same way as suggested in the final question of Assignment 72, above.

89

Handel (1685-1759)

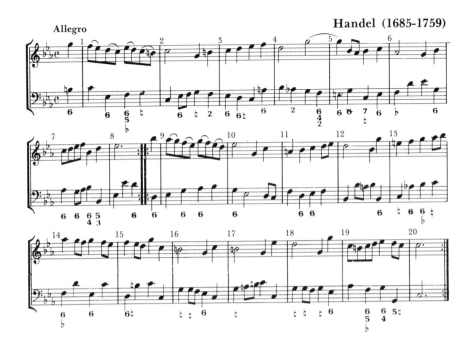

1. Which instrument plays the melody in this piece? How does this instrument produce its sounds?

2. Which instruments play the accompaniment? How are the sounds produced on each of these instruments?

3. Although the music printed above contains all the notes which Handel provides, only the melody and bass-line are included. Explain the meaning of the figures below the bass-line.

4. Which key does Handel choose as his tonic key for this piece?

5. (a) On which note of the scale does the melody begin? Is it: the tonic, subdominant, dominant, or leading-note?
   (b) On which of these does the melody end?

6. Using technical names as above, describe (i) the first two notes and (ii) the final two notes of the bass-line.

7. To which key has the music modulated by bar 8? How is this new key related to the tonic key?

8. Through which key does the music pass during bars 11 and 12?

9. With which kind of cadence does this piece end?

10. Describe the intervals which occur between these notes in the bass:
    (a) the first two notes of bar 12;
    (b) the first two notes of bar 14;
    (c) the last two notes of bar 16.

11. Which form or design does Handel use to build up this piece?

12. This is a movement from a longer work. Is that work likely to be a sonata, a quartet, a concerto, or a symphony?

Assignment 75   'Swiss Yodelling Song' from *Façade*   **Walton (1902-1983)**

Cor anglais   flute   piccolo

Make a copy of the score above. Then, as you listen to the music, add the following details to your score.

1. Beneath the opening tune, write the name of the instrument you hear playing.

2. Write   *pizzicato bass*   below the first bar where this occurs.

3. Write   *flute*   below the bar where this phrase is played:

Afterwards, in brackets, write whichever of these terms is suitable:
    legato staccato

4. Mark ✱ below the correct beat of each of the four bars where you hear a cymbal being struck.

5. Draw a bracket above the bars where this music is heard:

Below each bar, write the name of the instrument which plays.

6. Write   *tr*   below any bars where you hear a tambourine being shaken.

7. Below bar 19, write the name of the instrument which plays the trill.

8. Below bar 22, write the name of the instrument which plays the high, rather strident phrase.

9. At the beginning of your score, write a suitable Italian tempo marking.

10. Walton describes *Façade* as 'An Entertainment', and writes this music very much 'tongue in cheek'. Beneath your score, mention some of the musical jokes – the humorous touches – which he includes here.

Assignment 76   'Les Dragons d'Alcala' (The Dragons of Alcala)   Bizet (1838-1875)
from the opera, *Carmen*

1. Which instruments play the tune of the first section of this piece?
    Explain a 2 printed above the first bar of the tune.

2. Which percussion instrument crisply accompanies the tune?

3. Which other instruments join in the accompaniment? How are they
    played?

4. In which bar does the second section of the piece begin?

5. Which two families of instruments play alternately in this section
    of the piece?

6. At which bar does the opening tune return? Which instrument plays it?

7. Which instrument plays a *staccato* accompaniment?

8. At which bar is a percussion instrument next heard?

9. Bizet rounds off his piece with a *coda*, beginning at bar 79. Name the
    four solo instruments which play in turn during the coda.

10. Which musical form or design does Bizet use to build up this piece?

Bartók designs this movement in ternary (three-part) form: $A^1 B\ A^2$.
The first part, A^1, is built up in eleven sections of music in which
the strings of the orchestra alternate with the solo piano. Here is
a plan of this part of the music, with approximate timings in seconds:

1	2	3	4	5	6	7	8	9	10	11
Strings (77″)	Piano (20″)	Strings (20″)	Piano (20″)	Strings (15″)	Piano (20″)	Strings (14″)	Piano (37″)	Strings (7″)	Piano (26″)	Strings (20″)

The music of Section 1 begins: In Section 2 the pianist plays this music:

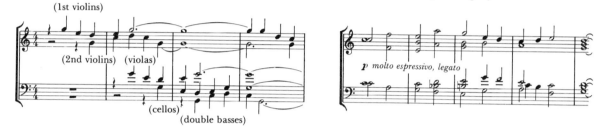

Listen to this music and answer these questions:

(a)   Suggest a dynamic marking, and also an Italian tempo marking, to
match the music of Section 1. Is it played *legato*, or *staccato*?

(b)   Which of these words matches the musical style of Section 2?
coda; *chorale*; *canon*; *recitative*.

(c)   Which of these melodic shapes matches the first four notes played
by the pianist in Section 4?

(i) ⌒   (ii) ⌒   (iii) ⌒

(d)   Which of these words would appear below the music of Section 6?
ritenuto; *accelerando*; *tacet*; *crescendo*; *diminuendo*.

(e)   Below the music of Section 8 Bartók adds these markings: *ff* *sfz*
Which Italian words do these represent? What does each one mean?

(f)   Describe the mood of the music of Section 10.

(g)   Section 11 is based on the same musical idea as Section 1. What is
the main difference in the way it is presented in this final section?

Listen to the music again, answering these questions:

(h)   In Section 1, the groups of strings enter with the same phrase in
imitation. What do you notice about this phrase as it is presented
by the second violins, and the double basses?

(i)   What contrast in *texture* is there between the music presented by
the strings, and the music presented by the piano?

(j)   Note down any other contrasts which Bartók introduces during this
music.

(k)   In which of the sections of music featuring the piano are discords
most noticeable?

(l)   What is a *concerto*? Mention and describe two different types.

Timechart of composers and countries

Medieval   **Renaissance**   **Baroque**

1500   1600   1700

Medieval

800   900   1000   1100   1200   1300   1400   1500

...ARS ANTIQUA > < ARS NOVA ...

Plainchant . . .

Organum

(parallel)   (free)   (melismatic) (Notre Dame composers)

Léonin . . .   . . .

Pérotin . . .   . . .

Trouvères

Troubadours

Dunstable c1390–1453

Dufay 1400–1474

Machaut 1300–1377

Landini c1325–1397

America	
Austria	
Bohemia	
Czechoslovakia	
Denmark	
England	Tallis c1505–1585 Byrd 1543–1623 Morley c1557–1602 Bull c1563–1628 Dowland 1563–1626 Weelkes 1576–1623 Gibbons 1583–1625 Purcell 1659–1695 Clarke c1674
Finland	
France	Lully 1632–1687 Couperin
Germany	Schütz 1585–1672
Netherlands	Josquin des Prez c1440–1521 Lassus c1532–1594
Italy	Palestrina c1525–1594 G. Gabrieli c1555–1612 Monteverdi 1567–1643 Corelli 1653–1713 A. Scarlatti 1660–1725

1450   1500   1600   1700

1700   1800   1900   2000

Hungary

Liszt 1811–1886

Bartók 1881–1945

Kodály 1882–1967

Norway

Grieg 1843–1907

Poland

Chopin 1810–1849

Penderecki born 1933–

Spain

Albeniz 1860–1909

Falla 1876–1946

USSR   Russia

Borodin 1833–1887

Prokofiev 1891–1953

Mussorgsky 1839–1881

Stravinsky 1882–1971

Tchaikovsky 1840–1893

Shostakovich 1906–1975

Rimsky-Korsakov 1844–1908

Rachmaninov 1873–1943

Ives 1874–1954

Copland born 1900–

Cage born 1912–

Haydn 1732–1809

Bruckner 1824–1896

Mozart 1756–1791

J. Strauss 1825–1899

Schubert   1797–1828

Mahler 1860–1911

Schoenberg 1874–1951

Webern 1883–1945

Berg 1885–1935

J. Stamitz 1717–1757

Smetana 1824–1884

Dvořák 1841–1904

Janáček 1854–1928

Nielsen 1865–1931

Elgar 1857–1934

Delius 1862–1934

Vaughan Williams 1872–1958

Holst 1874–1934

Walton 1902–1983

Tippett born 1905–

Britten 1913–1976

Sibelius 1865–1957

Berlioz 1803–1869

Messiaen born 1908–

Bizet 1835–1875

–1707

Debussy 1862–1918

Boulez born 1925–

Rameau 1683–1764

Ravel 1875–1937

J.C. Bach 1735–1782

Wagner 1813–1883

Bach 1685–1750

Beethoven 1770–1827

Brahms 1833–1897

Handel 1685–1759

Weber 1786–1826

R. Strauss 1864–1949

Gluck 1714–1787

Mendelssohn   1809–1847

Hindemith 1895–1963

C.P.E. Bach 1714–1788

Schumann 1810–1856

Stockhausen born 1928–

Rossini 1792–1868

Verdi 1813–1901

Puccini 1858–1924

Vivaldi 1678–1741

Berio born 1925–

D. Scarlatti 1685–1757

1668–1733

1700   1800   1900   2000

Index